SELECTIONS FROM CANADIAN POETS

Literature of Canada

Poetry and Prose in Reprint

Douglas Lochhead, General Editor

Selections from Canadian Poets

Edward Hartley Dewart

Introduction by Douglas Lochhead

UNIVERSITY OF TORONTO PRESS

Toronto and Buffalo
Printed in Canada
ISBN 0-8020-1952-8 (cloth)
ISBN 0-8020-6176-1 (paper)
ISBN Microfiche 0-8020-0295-1
LC 72-91691

Preface

Yes, there is a Canadian literature. It does exist. Part of the evidence to support these statements is presented in the form of reprints of the poetry and prose of the authors included in this series. Much of this literature has been long out of print. If the country's culture and traditions are to be sampled and measured, both in terms of past and present-day conditions, then the major works of both our well-known and our lesser-known writers should be available for all to buy and read. The Literature of Canada series aims to meet this need. It shares with its companion series, The Social History of Canada, the purpose of making the documents of the country's heritage accessible to an increasingly large national and international public, a public which is anxious to acquaint itself with Canadian literature – the writing itself – and also to become intimate with the times in which it grew.

DL

Edward Hartley Dewart, 1828-1903

Douglas Lochhead

Introduction

When his anthology *Selections from Canadian Poets* was published Edward Hartley Dewart was thirty-six years of age, a Methodist minister on the St Johns circuit, Canada East, and an essayist and poet in his own right. Five years later, in 1869, he became editor of the *Christian Guardian*, described as the 'principal organ of the Methodist Church in Canada' with offices in Toronto. But Dewart's own writing career began early. His biographical sketch in Morgan's *The Canadian Men and Women of the Time* reveals that 'his first literary attempt of importance was an essay against the use of tobacco by Christians, which won for him a gold watch against a number of competitors.'[1]

It is important to know something about Canada's first poetry anthologist. Evidently he held firm views throughout his ministerial and editorial career as well. 'A very Rupert in debate' was how the Reverend Dr Withrow described him. Another fellow cleric tells us something more. 'His opinions while in process of formation are like the molten metal, susceptible to pressure, but when once formed, like the hardened steel,' said the Reverend Dr J.S. Ross. Dewart's decision to express his feelings about Canadian poetry in the 1860s resulted in a selection of poetry which he supported with one of this country's firmest and most perceptive literary documents. His introduction, which is reprinted here, is also, as Gordon Roper has indicated, 'a classical argument for the need of a national literature to help build a sense of national identity.'[2]

It is possible to read Dewart's introduction and selection of poetry within its nineteenth-century Canadian setting. But to attempt this is somewhat perilous, because one tends to forget that struggles for identity were continuing, say, in England, and were in an advanced state of fermentation in the United States. One need only be aware that in the years 1862 to 1863, while Dewart was compiling his anthology in Montreal and St Johns, there were being published in England such authors as Matthew Arnold *(On Translating Homer)*, George Borrow *(Wild Wales)*, Charles Darwin *(On the Contrivances by which Orchids are Fertilized)*, George Eliot *(Romola)*, George Meredith *(Modern Love)*, John Ruskin *(Unto This Last)*, Charles Swinburne *(Dead Love)*, and Anthony Trollope *(Orley Farm)*, all in 1862; and in 1863 Mrs Gaskell *(A Dark Night's Work*, *Sylvia's Lovers*, and *Crowley Castle)*, Charles Kingsley *(Water Babies)*, John Stuart Mill *(Utilitarianism)*, and William Makepeace Thackeray *(Roundabout Papers)*. During the same years, in the United States, were published Julia Ward Howe *(Battle Hymn of the Republic)*, Nathaniel Hawthorne *(Our Old Home)*, Jean Ingelow *(Poems)*, Abraham Lincoln *(Gettysburg Address)*, James Wadsworth Longfellow *(Tales of a Wayside Inn)*, and Henry Thoreau *(Excursions*, 1863, *Maine Woods* and *Cape Cod*, 1864).

Many of these selected titles of poetry, fiction, philosophy, theology, science, and art appeared first in periodicals. It was a century, and in the 1860s particularly, of prolific writers, of wide distribution of periodicals and books, and of advances in multiplying the printed word the publishing world had not dreamed of for four hundred years. Books of poetry were carried to Canada by new settlers, and those with literary interests made certain that they received additional reading material by mail. Except in the larger centres, bookselling was primitive, and Dewart has something to say about this state of affairs as well.

It was to be expected that in the face of the pressure and inspiration of growing literatures in other countries Canadians should examine their own poets, their own literature, not to mention their own identity (surely a continuing and never-ending process!). This is not to suggest that all Canadians in the mid-nineteenth century were omniverous readers conscious of the latest literary fashions in London, Paris, New York, and Boston, but some were, and sufficiently so to wake up, rub their eyes, and reach for the floor. It was a time to stand up to meet the morning. After all it was just a little over one hundred years since printing itself had begun in Canada (1751). One of the first of those to let his voice be heard on the subject of national literature was Edward Hartley Dewart.

Anyone compiling a contemporary anthology of poetry for publication immediately leaves himself open to criticism from many quarters. Anthologies reveal much. The standard of taste and degree of perception of the anthologist is reflected by his selections. The poems themselves demonstrate the fashions and ways of writing and reveal the creative heat or lack of it in a certain time and place. Whatever is set forth is fair game for readers and critics, not to mention any living poets who may have been left out.

Of all this Dewart was well aware. In his straightforward preface and introduction what he had to say was positive and realistic as far as his responsibilities were concerned. What was said by him in 1864 regarding the Canadian literary 'situation' has much relevance for today's Canadian poets, academics, compilers, and critics, as well as those frequenters of the new Grub streets in Toronto and Montreal.

As Canada's first anthologist, Dewart imposed upon himself a very real task, that of preserving the country's early poetry. In this he was understandably only partially successful, but what he did do, considering the time and place, was considerable. As he explains it:

> My object in compiling this volume has been to rescue from oblivion some of the floating pieces of Canadian authorship worthy of preservation in a more permanent form...

Dewart recognized that he was living in a time of unprecedented newspaper publication and that much poetry which he read would never appear again unless he played the role of rescuer. His role was clear. He did indeed save many poems from oblivion, but it is only right to point out that in those nineteenth-century newspapers and periodicals which have survived there are many poems still to be collected and given the attention they deserve.

It is estimated that there were approximately 400 newspapers, daily, tri-weekly, semi-weekly, weekly, and monthly publications in all of the country in 1865.[3] About two-thirds of these were located in the Canadas, East and West. In the Canadas alone, with a population of over two and one-half million, there was no lack of outlets for poets. For the most part newspaper editors of the nineteenth century were kindly disposed to poets and regular poetry columns were not uncommon.

Such statistics provide more proof, if it is needed, to support the observation of Northrop Frye that indeed 'all the evidence ... points to a highly articulate and argumentative society in nineteenth-century Canada.'[4] It has been suggested above that in Great Britain and the United States the forum for argument, poetry, prose, and every form of literary expression was in a high state of articulation as well. Television and radio were still to come. People only read and some believed what they saw in the newspapers.

Before looking at Dewart's introduction and selection of poems it might be worthwhile to attempt to recreate something of the atmosphere of the country's leading metropolis and literary centre, Montreal. For surely it would have been in that city and in St Johns some fifty miles away that Dewart gathered his poems and met the poets and editors whose help he acknowledges.

Eyewitness accounts of Montreal in the pre-Confederation years are filled with descriptions of hotels, offices, stations, bridges, wharves, and industries. More impersonal sources such as almanacs, yearbooks, and newspapers also help to reveal Montreal as a city where business was well established both locally and with national headquarters of financial enterprises which had strong international affiliations. It was the country's place of real wealth. Painters, photographers, writers, and publishers gathered there and combined to make it the major centre of culture, certainly of literary activity. One source of information alone, *The British North American Almanac and Annual Record for the Year 1864...*, in its advertisements as well as its hard statistical facts provides sufficient evidence that Montreal was the focus of major business, and was the educational and cultural capital of the country.

It is not very difficult to imagine the Reverend Mr Dewart travelling to Montreal in those busy pre-Confederation years in the course of fulfilling his clerical duties and literary pursuits. No doubt he would stay with friends or at one of the many hotels in downtown Montreal. It would be relatively easy for him to meet with newspaper editors, find out from them the addresses of poets whose work had appeared in their columns and to set in motion the 'extensive correspondence' to which he refers in his preface. It would be interesting to discover if the 'Dewart Papers' do exist and to piece together the day-by-day account of Dewart's anthology-in-progress. No doubt his visits to Montreal did much to provide a change from his church duties on the St Johns circuit, and to allow him to see at first hand the workings of newspaper offices and book publishers, not the least of whom was John Lovell, printer and publisher, whose name appears on the title-page of the anthology. Such experience probably influenced those who selected Dewart for the editorship of the *Christian Guardian* five years later.

What of the anthology itself? It was the first attempt to make a selection of our native literature and for this Dewart has been widely commended. What has received most attention from reader-critics is his introduction, which has been much praised for its foresight, its endeavour to come to grips with the influences of other literatures, mainly English, and its realization that something called 'colonialism' was a major shaping force of Canadian poets and their poems. These among other things made Dewart's whole endeavour not only worthwhile, but deserving of reprinting because much of it applies to Canada today. Dewart is no apologist. As a strong advocate of Confederation he *loved* his country. His love embraced a firm faith in its future, its resources, its 'mysterious depths,' and above all its people as Canadians – people who would not be human or Canadian if they did not maintain some ties with the countries and cultures from which they came.

As the reader will discover for himself, the links with other countries as expressed by the poets in this book are close and moving. Out of these deeply felt emotions there is seen to be a shared concern to express what might be described as the 'now' and the 'place,' but often, inevitably, in terms of the 'past' and the 'other place.' We search in vain in this anthology for any real attempt by our pre-Confederation poets to describe the natural setting, the close particulars of their day to day experience. Certainly the drawings of W.H. Bartlett,[5] executed some twenty years earlier, are adequate demonstration of one artist's difficulty in expressing himself in terms uninfluenced by his past experience. What we do find is an expression, not without concern for the 'self,' as some critics would maintain, but which also embraces a larger loyalty – religious, political, philosophical, and above all nationalistic.

Poets are not theologians, politicians, biologists, or philosophers, but by following their individual ways they write about these subjects, as one would expect, in poetic terms. The table of contents will reveal the wide diversity of subjects dealt with. But, in general, it may be said that Canadian poets, along with English and American poets, wrote for the most part on themes common to them all. Regional differences are discernible, but these are not that important. What *is* interesting is that in the nineteenth century, poetry, whatever the country of its origin, was good and bad, spectacular and dull, and of its place and time. It is our obligation to attempt to read and take it within its particular nineteenth-century mood, or as near to this as we are able. It is no easy task, but the poets here do endeavour to speak of their 'now' and 'place' in ways the reader will warm to.

Accidents, or whatever, of history made Canada a country of English, Scottish, Irish, and French, and the nineteenth-century poets, if one takes this particular anthology as representative, were determined to find themselves, to maintain links with their homelands and with their past traditions. Their past history was important to them and they were not afraid to say so and to attempt to find themselves within their individual tradition but in a new place, this place whose physical forces were strange to them. They wrote, not so much about it, but freely and forcefully against this new backdrop to their suddenly transplanted lives. Perhaps much of what they did *not* say, for example about their daily lives, is important simply because it is not there. What faced these transplants was an adjustment to the new country's blood using the roots and traditions which were implanted in them. Religion, eighteenth- and nineteenth-century notions of literature and literary convention, are evident. What is obvious, too, in the long poems of the nineteenth century, is the poets' strong sense of drama, not only as recorders of it, but as participants. The relatively large number of long poems written by Canadian poets illustrates this new-found identity of which they were aware and which they sought to make clear to themselves and their readers. This was their 'now' and very close and intimate it was.

Dewart anticipated adverse criticisms of his selection of poetry by attaching a clear and no-nonsense preface to his book. Financial considerations forced him to limit his choice and he makes a point of saying he is sorry if any readers are unhappy with his anthology. He decided upon the poems for the book, and in his own words: 'I have nothing to regret.' He finishes his preface by expressing the hope that he has been 'instrumental in awakening a more extensive interest in the Poets and Poetry of our *beloved* country...' The word 'beloved' is rarely used today in this context but one senses a revival and it does not seem out of place to this present-day reader.

It is tempting to quote or to paraphrase what the anthologist has to say in his 'Introductory Essay.' One must yield sometimes simply to emphasize the fact that much of what Dewart saw fit to write in 1864 is applicable now.

Dewart begins his 'Essay' by disposing of the old chestnut, still uncomfortably with us, that because so many poetry and prose works have already been published there is need for no more. Worriers about the information explosion in 1864 could be classified as 'illiterate and unreflecting.' So could those who would argue that Canada received enough intellectual nourishment from other countries that it was a waste of time for native writers to bother expressing themselves.

On the first page of his 'Essay' perhaps the most prominent statement reads as follows:

> *A national literature is an essential element in the formation of national character.*

It appears in italics here because it sums up Dewart's own strong feelings about poetry and is, I suggest, the pivotal point around which his whole essay rides. Poets are national heroes in other countries because their important role is recognized. But not yet in Canada. Not yet.

In discussing the cold and indifferent reception given to poetry in Canada, the essayist destroys another old and flagging notion – that poetry was not written in Canada because its new settlers were too involved in making homes for themselves to worry about such things. Dewart is quick to point out that it is not that nineteenth-century Canadians are without the ability or the energy but because of the prevailing opinion that poetry is but a 'tissue of misleading fancies' and that general public taste is not yet developed and capable of recognizing the value of poetry. These are some of the 'subtle and powerful antagonisms' working against it.

The public remains unaware of what poetry is made. His fellow Canadians do not recognize, to quote Dewart, that:

> Poetry is the medium by which the emotions of beauty, joy, admiration, reverence, harmony, or tenderness kindled in the poet-soul, in communion with Nature and God, is conveyed to the souls of others.

This was poetry as Dewart felt it. If people looked down their noses at the pursuit of poetry because it yielded no tangible benefits, then that was too bad. If readers did not appreciate the fact that such themes as 'beauty, truth, the human soul, the works of God, the mystery of life...' were not appropriate to compress into rigid and firm forms of speech, then that was also too bad.

In describing what poetry does, Dewart is convincing, enthusiastic, and obviously at the peak of his message. His explanation that comes closest to today's readers is simply that poetry projects 'a new charm around common objects.'

Dewart is convinced that the majority of Canadians look upon the role of poet as something part-time, rather dubious at best, and altogether for the young and lazy. To Dewart the role of poet is noble and respectable. His realization that the country's colonial position is not helpful is expressed in terms of the reaction of the Canadian poet himself. There is no doubt in Dewart's mind that the native poet who sings of his own landscape will secure only contempt rather than sympathy and understanding.

Canadian poets receive a word of advice from the anthologist as well. Poetry is hard work and only those who recognize this fact will go beyond parlour fantasies. Dewart praises those poets represented in his book who have dealt with Canadian subjects. Of these Charles Sangster is ranked first in importance and there are others such as Alexander McLachlan, Charles Heavysege, and Susanna Moodie. In all Dewart includes one hundred and seventy-two poems by forty-eight poets in his selection.

If Canada is not a country with a long past, Dewart continues, this lack of mythology could be a good thing. We stand unshackled in a place where freedom of thought is ours, where there are 'broader spheres of action.' When he concludes by describing this country with its 'grand and gloomy forests,' by gloomy he means magnificent, mysterious. Here, in this Methodist voice, there is no hint of 'fear' or 'terror' of the wilderness. Is there a hint of the 'garrison mentality' in this nineteenth-century spokesman? In this case it would seem to be the 'cathedral mentality' with all the openness, freedom, and mystery implied in, and associated with, that phrase. 'Cathedral' is the word, not 'garrison.'

Here is an excerpt from a contemporary review of *Selections from Canadian Poets* which appeared in the *Quebec Chronicle:*

> This book ought at least to convince those who are not disposed to believe – and we hold that there are many even among the best informed – that we have in this Canada a few writers of verse whose productions, had they appeared in British or American periodicals would have won for their authors literary renown of no mean order...
>
> What Mr Dewart has done he has done well. His choice has been most judicious: his introductory essay affords ample food for thought to those who take an interest in our

literature; his critical notes are always in excellent taste and his preface at once fully explains his subject...

He is certainly entitled to the lasting gratitude of all who take an interest in Canadian literature.

In this anthology the poems are divided in three general sections: 'Sacred and Reflective,' 'Descriptive and National,' and 'Miscellaneous Pieces.' These are not arbitrary divisions, as will be obvious, and the reader may dip into a wide selection of Canadian pre-Confederation poetry wherever he chooses. Dewart does indeed deserve our gratitude.

NOTES

1 Henry James Morgan, *The Canadian Men and Women of the Time* (Toronto 1898), 267
2 Robert Fulford, David Godfrey, and Abraham Rotstein, eds, *Read Canadian* (Toronto 1972), 210
3 Peter B. Waite, *The Life and Times of Confederation, 1864-1867* (Toronto 1962), 6
4 Carl F. Klinck, gen. ed., *Literary History of Canada: Canadian Literature in English* (Toronto 1965), 831
5 Nathaniel Parker Willis, *Canadian Scenery Illustrated. From Drawings by W.H. Bartlett...* (London 1842)

Selections from Canadian Poets with Occasional Critical and Biographical Notes and an Introductory Essay on Canadian Poetry

SELECTIONS

FROM

CANADIAN POETS;

WITH OCCASIONAL

CRITICAL AND BIOGRAPHICAL NOTES,

AND AN

Introductory Essay on Canadian Poetry.

BY

EDWARD HARTLEY DEWART.

Montreal:
PRINTED BY JOHN LOVELL, ST. NICHOLAS STREET.
1864.

CONTENTS.

Miscellaneous Pieces.

PREFACE.

My object in compiling this volume has been to rescue from oblivion some of the floating pieces of Canadian authorship worthy of preservation in a more permanent form; and to direct the attention of my fellow-countrymen to the claims of Canadian poetry. The fact that I entered on an untrodden path, without any way-marks to guide me, necessarily caused me a vast amount of labor, and an extensive correspondence; as, in many instances, both poets and poetry had to be discovered by special research. This will, I hope, be duly considered by readers in judging of the work, should it be found less perfect than they had anticipated.

As I do not wish to be judged by a wrong standard, I must remind my readers that this is not "a work on the Poets and Poetry of Canada." Such a work may be highly desirable and necessary; and there is valuable material, in the poetic effusions of the past fifty years, with which to enrich such a work. But this collection makes no pretension to such a character: it is simply "SELECTIONS FROM CANADIAN POETS." With the hope of enhancing the interest and usefulness of the work, I have subjoined occasional brief notes; but the plan and scope of the work precluded any lengthy biographical sketches. It is easy for persons who have neither literary nor financial responsibility, to suggest changes in the plan of such a work. But the same persons might, in a different position, fail to act on their own suggestions. To those who may feel disappointed, because selections are not made from their poetry, I have no apology to offer. An immense quantity of verse, much of it of high merit, has passed under my notice. Financial reasons compelled me to limit the size of the volume. I could not put in everything that I approved of. I have made a selection, according to the best of my judgment, without partiality, or sectional feeling of any kind. If any are dissatisfied with me, I am sorry; but, conscious of the integrity of my motives, I have nothing to regret. Nearly all the pieces in this volume are published by special permission of the authors; and many of them have never been published before.

My warmest thanks are due to the authors for the courtesy and liberality with which, without exception, they placed their poems at my disposal; and to editors of newspapers throughout the country for their friendly notice of my project. They are also due to the subscribers—many of whom I recognize as personal friends—for their confidence and patronage, by which I have been encouraged to place the work before the public. Should it secure their approbation, and be instrumental in awakening a more extensive interest in the Poets and Poetry of our beloved country, my humble labors will be amply rewarded.

St. Johns, Canada East, Jan., 1864.

INTRODUCTORY ESSAY.

Only the illiterate and unreflecting adopt the sentiment, that, because more books have been already produced than can possibly be read in the compass of the longest life, to increase the number of books or the quantity of literature, is undesirable and unnecessary. The literature of the world is the foot-prints of human progress; and unless all progress should cease, and mental paralysis arrest all human activity, these way-marks shall continue to be erected along the pathway of the vanishing years. Whatever is discovered as new in the records of creation, in the capacities and relations of things, in the history of the mind's operations, or in the forms of thought and imagery by which in its higher moods soul speaks to soul, will always demand some suitable embodiment in literature.

Equally shallow and reprehensible is the idea, very widely entertained, that, because we can procure sufficient quantities of mental aliment from other lands, it is superfluous to make any attempt to build up a literature of our own. A national literature is an essential element in the formation of national character. It is not merely the record of a country's mental progress: it is the expression of its intellectual life, the bond of national unity, and the guide of national energy. It may be fairly questioned, whether the whole range of history presents the spectacle of a people firmly united politically, without the subtle but powerful cement of a patriotic literature. On the other hand, it is easy to show, that, in the older countries of the world, the names of distinguished poets, enshrined in the national heart, are the watchwords of national union; and it has become a part of the patriotism of the people to honor and love their memory. To mention the names of Shakspere and Burns, alone justifies this assertion. It is to be regretted that the tendency to sectionalism and disintegration, which is the political weakness of Canada, meets no counterpoise in the literature of the country. Our French fellow-countrymen are much more firmly united than the English colonists; though their literature is more French than Canadian, and their bond of union is more religious than literary or political. Besides, if the conditions of human existence and progress are changed, by the lapse of time, the advances of physical and mental science, difference of social and political institutions, and geographical situation, it would be absurd to suppose that such changes demanded no corresponding modifications in the teachings of literature.

There is probably no country in the world, making equal pretensions to intelligence and progress, where the claims of native literature are so little felt, and where every effort in poetry has been met with so much coldness and indifference, as in Canada. And what is more to be deprecated than neglect of our most meritorious authors, is the almost universal absence of interest and faith in all indigenous literary productions, and the undisturbed satisfaction with a state of things, that, rightly viewed, should be regarded as a national reproach. The common method of accounting for this by the fact that almost the whole community is engaged in the pursuit of the necessaries and comforts of life, and that comparatively few possess wealth and leisure, to enable them to give much time or thought to the study of poetry and kindred subjects, is by no means satisfactory. This state of things is doubtless unfavorable to the growth of poetry; but there are other causes less palpable, which exert a more subtle and powerful antagonism.

Nothing so seriously militates against the growth and extension of our poetic literature, as the low and false conceptions which extensively prevail respecting the nature and influence of poetry itself. Many regard it as a tissue of misleading fancies, appealing chiefly to superstitious credulity, a silly and trifling thing, the product of the imagination when loosed from the control and direction of reason. These misconceptions may have arisen from a natural incapacity for appreciating the truths which find their highest embodiment in poetry, from familiarity with low styles, or from the frequency with which verse has been degraded to be the vehicle of low and debasing thought. But whatever be their origin, they are false and misleading. They ignore the essential unity of the mind. Poetry is not the product of any one faculty of the mind: it is the offspring of the whole mind, in the full exercise of all its faculties, and in its highest moods of sympathy, with the truths of the worlds of mind and matter. It is not some artificial distortion of thought and language by a capricious fancy: it has its foundation in the mental constitution which our Creator has given us. As fragrance to the sense of smell, music to the ear, or beauty to the eye, so is poetry to the sensibilities of the heart. It ministers to a want of our intellectual nature. This is the secret of its power, and the pledge of its perpetuity. An able American writer observes with great truth and beauty: "It was spontaneous in its growth, and native in its origin. It arose from those immutable principles of harmony, established originally by Him who strung that invisible harp in the nature of man, and tuned accordant the mightier instruments of the universe around him. It is not therefore dependent on the mutations of human caprice and fashion; nor is it superseded by the discoveries and improvements in society." Poetry is the medium by which the emotions of beauty, joy, admiration, reverence, harmony, or tenderness kindled in the poet-soul, in communion with Nature and God, is conveyed to the souls of others. As there are rhymesters who have no true poetic feeling, so there are many who are not gifted with the power of giving expression to the emotions which throb for utterance at the heart. The influence of beauty or grandeur, moral and physical, "they feel, but cannot speak." To this feeling, which exists in a stronger or weaker degree in all minds, Poetry appeals. Where this tongueless poetry of the heart has no existence, or exists in a very feeble degree, the conditions for appreciating poetic excellence are wanting. As well might the blind judge of beauty, or the deaf of music, as such to judge of poetry. Let no one therefore speak of their disregard for poetry as if it indicated a superiority to ordinary weakness: it is an imperfection, that may be endured as a misfortune, but should never be flaunted as a virtue.

Persons of this class often assume, that because poetry has not a low tangible utility, capable of being comprehended by sordid minds, it is vain and useless. But there are many things in nature to which God has given the power of increasing human happiness and well-being, though they do not impart what may be called tangible benefits or gross enjoyment. Of this character is the pleasure received from the beauty and fragrance of a flower-garden; the murmur and sparkle of a pebbly stream; a mountain-lake sleeping among the hills; a tranquil evening, when the sunset-flush of departing day gilds every object with golden lustre; or the soul-soothing strains of melodious music. It is not without design that God has spread these sources of pleasure so thickly around us. To persons of sensibility, they yield a deep and speechless joy, vastly purer and more elevating than any form of sordid or sensual gratification. Now, poetry may be regarded as occupying in the world of mind, a place and a purpose analogous to scenes of beauty or grandeur in the material world. The useful and the beautiful are both from God. Each has its appropriate sphere. They are not antagonistic: the one is the complement of the other. And although poetry may not be the vehicle of hard jagged facts, it may convey truths of greater depth and power than are embodied in granite syllogisms or definitions. The greatest truths are not those that are most readily and flippantly expressed in words. In the language of an eminent English divine, "what is gained in clearness is lost in breadth." When we fancy we have compressed a truth into some very clear and definite form of words, some of its deeper meanings have escaped: like pressed grapes, the substance may be there, but the wine is gone.

If the indefiniteness of poetic language and thought be urged as an objection, it is easy to show that this indefiniteness belongs essentially to the subjects with which it converses. Beauty, truth, the human soul, the works of God, the mystery of life,—are not themes whose significance can be easily compressed into rigid and superficial forms of speech. Let it not therefore be supposed, that because poetry is not fruitful in direct and palpable results, that its influence is small or its mission unimportant. It soothes human sorrow. It ministers to human happiness. It fires the soul with noble and holy purpose. It expands and quickens. It refines the taste. It opens to us the treasures of the universe, and brings us into closer sympathy with all that is beautiful, and grand, and true. It sheds a new charm around common objects; because it unveils their spiritual relations, and higher and deeper typical meanings. And it educates the mind to a quicker perception of the harmony, grandeur, and truth disclosed in the works of the Creator. The history of poetry is a sufficient rebuke to those who speak slightingly of its influence. We know of no period in the world's history where it was not a power either for good or evil. It has exerted a mighty influence on some of the leading minds of every age; to say nothing of the "hymns of faith and hope," that have, in every period and sphere in the history of the church, proved, in life and in death, a source of strength and consolation to its members. If, in many instances, this sacred gift has been linked with folly, scepticism, and licentiousness, this did not arise from any native tendency of poetry itself. In such instances, Poetry is false to her mission; and gifted men are wicked in spite of their gifts. But this is not her native sphere. It is the beloved son, far from his true home, feeding swine. And even in those melancholy cases where poetic gifts are perverted and degraded, there are seen, like grains of gold amid the dross, outbursts of indignation against wrong, gleams of admiration for virtue, and gushes of tender sympathy for human suffering, that seem like the protest of Poesie, in her thraldom, against a forced and unnatural divorcement from beauty, purity, and truth.

These views respecting the dignity of poetry will enable us to take higher and truer views of the work and mission of him to whom God has given this "vision and faculty divine." How low and unworthy are the popular conceptions of the Poet's work and character! The many have thought of him as a mere rhymer of idle and foolish fancies, deserving censure because not better employed. Of course those who cherished false and degrading views of poetry, had equally false and unworthy views of the character of a Poet. But the Poet's work is a lofty and sacred work. It is not merely to wreath garlands around the brow of Beauty, to cover Vice with graceful drapery, or to sing the praise of Bacchus and Venus in Anacreontic ditties: but to refine and elevate the spiritual in our nature; to sing of earth's woes and sufferings, and pour the balm of a tender sympathy into sorrow-stricken hearts; to unveil, in its true deformity, the selfish cruelty of man to his fellow-man; and to portray the loveliness of unselfish benevolence, piety, and truth. The true Poet does for us what the eagle is said to do for her young, bears us aloft, and teaches us to fly. On the wings of his soaring spirit, we are borne into higher and more ethereal regions of thought, than our own unaided pinions could attain; where the silent forms of inanimate Nature awake to life, and pour their melodious eloquence upon the soul. He stands as a priest at Nature's high altars to expound her symbolic language, to unveil her hidden beauty, to dispense her sacred lessons, and to lead the mind up from the tokens of his presence on earth to the Great Father of all in heaven.

Our colonial position, whatever may be its political advantages, is not favorable to the growth of an indigenous literature. Not only are our mental wants supplied by the brain of the Mother Country, under circumstances that utterly preclude competition; but the majority of persons of taste and education in Canada are emigrants from the Old Country, whose tenderest affections cling around the land they have left. The memory of the associations of youth, and of the honored names that have won distinction in every department of human activity, throws a charm around everything that comes from their native land, to which the productions of our young and unromantic country can put forth no claim.

When the poets of other countries sing of the birds and flowers, the mountains and streams, of those lands, whose history is starred with deathless names, and rich with the mellow and hazy light of romance, every reference to those immortal types of beauty or grandeur commands sympathy and admiration. But let any Canadian bard presume to think that the wild-flowers which formed the garlands of his sunny childhood, the sweet song-birds that sang him to sleep in infancy, or the magnificent lakes, forests, and rivers of his native land, are as worthy of being enshrined in lyric numbers, and capable of awaking memories of days as bright, associations as tender, and scenery as beautiful, as ever was sung by hoary harper of the olden time, and he is more likely to secure contempt than sympathy or admiration. Things that are hoary with age, and dim in their distance, from us, are more likely to win veneration and approval, while whatever is near and familiar loses in interest and attraction. There is a large class of persons who could scarcely conceive it possible that a Canadian lyric might have as deep and true feeling as those they have most admired; or that a Canadian Poet might be as highly gifted as some of the favourite names who are crowned with the wreaths of unfading fame. And yet such things are not altogether inconceivable. But if a Milton or a Shakspere, was to arise among us, it is far from certain that his merit would be recognized. The mass of readers find it easier and safer to re-echo the approbation of others,—to praise those whom all praise,—than to form an intelligent and independent judgment of their own.

Other antagonistic influences have not been wanting. Religious intolerance is always unjust to talent that does not belong to its party, and pronounce its watchwords. There are many who take great credit for liberality, so blinded by bigotry, that with them it would be enough to condemn the most meritorious work, that it sprung from any quarter, from which it was not in accordance with their canonized prejudices to believe anything good could come.

The indiscriminate praise, by the press, of some writers, in which, whatever their merit, the dross was largely mixed with the pure ore, has tended to mislead the public, and to give the authors false notions of their talents and achievements. Booksellers, too, because they make surer sales and large profits on British and American works, which have already obtained popularity, seldom take the trouble to judge of a Canadian book on its merits, or use their influence to promote its sale. The chances are, that, whatever its merit, the author will be left to send his work around to the bookstores at his own expense, and leave it to be sold at his own risk, paying a liberal percentage for any copies that may be sold.

In pronouncing judgment on the character of our native poetry, the most partial critic must confess that it is extensively marked by crudity and imperfection. This is to some extent accounted for by the want of educational advantages incident to a new country. Many writers of undoubted genius have been deficient in that thorough literary culture essential to high artistic excellence. But in many instances this want of finish may be traced to want of application, resulting from a low estimate of poetry as an art. The adage, that "whatever is worth doing at all is worth doing well," has a special application here. There is no such dearth of poetry, as to warrant every unfledged bantling being thrust upon the public as a bird of Paradise. It would be well, if all who have contracted the habit of turning commonplace puerilities into rhyme "for their own amusement," would sacredly devote them to that purpose. Poesie, like Truth, will unveil her beauty and dispense her honors, only to those who love her with deep and reverential affection. Because no rules nor study can make a man a poet without genius, it does not follow that the most gifted may not be profited by a study of those principles that are illustrated in the works of the great masters of lyric harmony. Every true conception of poetry must regard it both as a sentiment and an art. The essence of poetry lies in the character of the thought. No dexterity of art can galvanize into poetry, low, puerile thought, destitute of pathos, beauty, and grandeur. But it is an error to infer from this that the character of the thought is everything, and the form in which it is expressed of little consequence. The difference between prose and poetry consists more in the form than in the essential nature of the thought. Every reader knows that noble and good sentiments may be so tamely expressed, as to produce aversion rather than pleasure. Much "religious poetry" and "hymns" painfully illustrate this. Themes which require the most masterly genius, are most frequently travestied by feeble incompetence. The careful selection of unhackneyed, elegant, and expressive words, and their arrangement in such forms as will produce musical harmony, are elements of success with which no genius can dispense.

If, as we have seen, the object of poetry is to convey to others the emotions and conceptions which thrill the poet's own soul, in his highest mental moods, it follows that the perfection of the medium to which these thoughts are committed, is a matter of essential importance. Poetry bears a close analogy to music, and appeals to the sense of harmony, as well as to the understanding. No really good poetry is deficient in metrical harmony. Hence we see the folly of the objection, sometimes urged against poetry, "that generally on being translated into prose it does not seem to contain much." This is assuming that the object of poetry is to convey knowledge of positive facts, and consequently judging it by a wrong standard. As well might we deny the beauty of a sparkling dew-drop, because on examination it is found to consist of common water; or the merit of a beautiful painting, because the colors to which it owes its fine effect, might be so mixed or arranged as to possess no charm or beauty.

To those who are best acquainted with the poetry of Canada, the wonder is, not that so little has been achieved, but that so much true poetry has been written, in spite of such unpropitious circumstances. For poetic fire, like its earthly type, requires vent in order to burn brightly. Some of our most gifted poets, after ineffectual efforts to gain the attention and approval of the public, have despairingly turned to more hopeful, though less congenial labors, feeling that their choicest strains fell on listless ears, and unsympathetic hearts.

Among those who have most courageously appealed to the reading public, and most largely enriched the poetic literature of Canada, the first place is due to CHARLES SANGSTER. The richness and extent of his contributions, the originality and descriptive power he displays, the variety of Canadian themes on which he has written with force and elegance, his passionate sympathy with the beautiful in Nature, and the chivalrous and manly patriotism which finds an utterance in his poems, fully vindicate his claim to a higher place in the regard of his countrymen, than he has yet obtained. ALEXANDER MCLACHLAN has also evinced that he possesses in a high degree the gift of song. In the opinion of many, he is the sweetest and most intensely human of all our Canadian bards. As Sangster and McLachlan are quite unlike, and each possesses a strongly marked individuality of his own, any comparison between them is inappropriate, and might be unfair to both. In elaborate elegance and wealth of descriptive power, in the success with which he has treated Canadian themes, and in something of Miltonic stateliness and originality of style, Sangster has certainly no equal in this country. But in strong human sympathy, in subtle appreciation of character, in deep natural pathos, and in those gushes of noble and manly feeling which awaken the responsive echoes of every true heart, McLachlan is equally peerless. That they should both be so little known to the reading public of Canada, is a matter of sincere regret. Taking into consideration the subtle delicacy of thought and elevation of style which distinguishes much of his poetry, it is not so difficult to understand why Sangster should be comparatively unappreciated by the great mass of readers; but that the sentiments of sympathy with humanity in all conditions, and the protests against every form of injustice and pretension, so simply and earnestly expressed in McLachlan's poetry, should secure so few admirers, is a fact that, in spite of all possible explanations, is by no means creditable to the taste or intelligence of Canada.

Enough however has already been achieved, to be an earnest of better things for the future. The philosophic subtlety and creative imagination of Heavysege,—the profound sensibility and exquisite musical harmony of Miss Vining,—the lofty aspirations and ringing energy of Miss Haight,—the delicate perception of beauty which breathes forth in the lyrics of Ascher,—the ardent human sympathy and tenderness of Mrs. Leprohon,—the calm beauty and attractive grace of Prof. Chapman,—the simple and graphic truthfulness of Mrs. Moodie,—the intense communion with Nature in her moods of quiet loveliness, which soothes and charms, in the musical strains of J. F. McDonnell,—the simple melodies of Miss Johnson, full of earnestness and deep religious feeling,—and many other names worthy of honorable mention, give a pledge to futurity that it will not always be Winter with Canadian poetry. Should the soft Spring breath of kindly appreciation warm the chilly atmosphere, flowers of greater luxuriance and beauty would soon blossom forth, to beautify and enrich our literature.

If these anticipations are not realized, it is not because there is anything in the country itself uncongenial to poetry. If we are deprived of many of the advantages of older countries, we have ample compensation in more unshackled freedom of thought, and broader spheres of action. Though poor in historic interest, our past is not altogether devoid of events capable of poetic treatment. But if Memory cannot draw rich materials for poetry from treasures consecrated to fame, Hope unfolds the loftier inspiration of a future bright with promise. If we cannot point to a past rich with historic names, we have the inspiring spectacle of a great country, in her youthful might, girding herself for a race for an honorable place among the nations of the world. In our grand and gloomy forests—in our brilliant skies and varied seasons—in our magnificent lakes and rivers—in our hoary mountains and fruitful valleys, external Nature unveils her most majestic forms to exalt and inspire the truly poetic soul; while human nature—especially human nature in its relation to the spiritual and divine—still presents an exhaustless mine of richest ore, worthy of the most exalted genius, and of the deepest human and spiritual knowledge.

SELECTIONS FROM CANADIAN POETS.

DAWN.

J. J. PROCTER.

Break o'er the sea! Break on the night!
Ever blessed and holy light;
Shed but one ray, but one joyous beam,
Wherever the eastern waters gleam—
But one small ray, for the night is dark,
And the ocean waits for the first bright spark;
Others are longing too for thee,
Break o'er the sea! Break o'er the sea!

O dawn! O rosy-fingered dawn!
Come up and herald another morn;
Come, till the dark mists fly away;
Come, till the night gives place to day;
Come where the deep black waters boom;
Come through the veil of the sullen gloom;
All things are longing, O light, for thee,
Break o'er the sea! Break o'er the sea!

O day! O happy happy day!
Chase the gloomy shadows away.
Though Nature's slumbers seem calm and deep,
There are those on earth who cannot sleep—

Those who in toil alone are blest—
Those who in labor alone find rest.
Hearts that are breaking have need of thee;
Break o'er the sea! Break o'er the sea!

O light! O tender tender light!
There came a cry through the live-long night;
Wherever a mortal foot has trod,
A cry of woe to a loving God,
From those who would drink of the fabled wave
That gives forgetfulness long as the grave:
Sorrowing souls have need of thee,
Break o'er the sea! Break o'er the sea!

O waves that were moaning all night long,
Break out, and join in the angels' song;
Thunder it out with shock on shock
Into the ears of the dull hard rock;
Whisper it low to the far-off strand
Where the ripplets lazily laugh on the sand,
Till earth shall echo from flower to tree,
Break o'er the sea! Break o'er the sea!

O type of the Everlasting Day!
Come from the East land far away;
The land whence once came a holy voice
Bidding all mourning hearts rejoice;
Come and recall its echoes now,
Flash on the darkened and sullen brow,
Bid all doubts and all sorrows flee,
Break o'er the sea! Break o'er the sea!

O sun, rise up from thy watery bed!
Rise till the shades of night have fled!
Sweep on, on thy mission, and linger not,
With rays of love, on each sacred spot
Where He, the Pure One, for sinners bled,
Where earth once covered her Maker's head—
He that made thee is calling to thee,
Break o'er the sea! break o'er the sea!

THE STARS.

CHARLES SANGSTER.

From Hesperus.

The Stars are heaven's ministers;
Right royally they teach
God's glory and omnipotence,
In wondrous lowly speech.
All eloquent with music, as
The tremblings of a lyre,
To him that hath an ear to hear
They speak in words of fire.

Not to learnèd sagas only
Their whisperings come down;
The monarch is not glorified
Because he wears a crown.
The humblest soldier in the camp
Can win the smile of Mars,
And 'tis the lowliest spirits hold
Communion with the stars.

Thoughts too refined for utterance,
　　Etherial as the air,
Crowd through the brain's dim labyrinths,
　　And leave their impress there;
As far along the gleaming void
　　Man's searching glances roll,
Wonder usurps the throne of speech,
　　But vivifies the soul.

O heaven-cradled mysteries,
　　What sacred paths ye've trod—
Bright, jewelled scintillations from
　　The chariot-wheels of God!
When in the spirit He rode forth,
　　With vast creative aim,
These were His footprints left behind,
　　To magnify His name!

GOD.

ALEX. M'LACHLAN.

Hail, Thou great mysterious being!
Thou the unseen yet all-seeing,
　　To Thee we call.
How can a mortal sing thy praise,
Or speak of all thy wondrous ways,
　　God over all!

God of the great old solemn woods,
God of the desert solitudes,
And trackless sea;
God of the crowded city vast,
God of the present and the past,
Can man know Thee?

God of the blue vault overhead,
Of the green earth on which we tread,
Of time and space.
God of the worlds which time conceals,
God of the worlds which death reveals,
To all our race.

God of the glorious realms of thought,
From which some simple hearts have caught
A ray divine:
And the songs which rouse the nations,
And the terrible orations,
Lord God are thine.

And all the forms of beauty rare,
Which toiling genius moulds with care,
Yea the sublime,
The sculptured forms of joy and woe,
By Thee were fashioned long ago,
In that far clime.

Far above earth and space and time,
Thou dwellest in thy heights sublime.

Beneath thy feet
The rolling worlds, the heavens, are spread
Glory infinite round Thee shed
Where angels meet.

From out thy wrath the earthquakes leap,
And shake the world's foundations deep,
Till Nature groans.
In agony the mountains call,
And ocean bellows throughout all
Her frightened zones.

But where thy smile its glory sheds,
The lilies lift their lovely heads,
And the primrose rare;
And the daisy, deck'd with pearls,
Richer than the proudest earls
On their mantles wear.

These thy preachers of the wild-wood
Keep they not the heart of childhood
Fresh within us still?
Spite of all our life's sad story,
There are gleams of Thee and glory
In the daffodil.

And old Nature's heart rejoices,
And the rivers lift their voices,
And the sounding sea;
And the mountains old and hoary,
With their diadems of glory,
Shout, Lord, to thee.

But though Thou art high and holy,
Thou dost love the poor and lowly,
With a love divine.
Love infinite, love supernal,
Love undying, love eternal,
Lord God are thine!

SHORT DAYS.*

ISIDORE G. ASCHER.

Over the pale crust of the ermine snow
The wind is roaming, chilled with winter's breath,
And the dim waning days seem touched with woe
For autumn's lingering death.

They gather varied hours in their train,
And lay them in the stillness of the past,
And o'er the fitful visions of the brain
Their broken shadows cast.

The evenings lengthen as the days subside,
Deepening and broadening to the peaceful night,
Like tender shadows, tempering as they hide
The noonday's garish light.

---

*This beautiful lyric, as well as the other pieces by the same author in this volume, is from "VOICES FROM THE HEARTH," published in 1863, by ISIDORE G. ASCHER, a young Jewish lawyer, of Montreal. Though not without occasional defects, which seem more the result of carelessness than of inability to do better, this volume reveals a subtle and delicate imagination, earnest and tender aspirations after the beautiful and the true, and, in several pieces, a rich musical harmony, which is full of promise of higher achievement in future, should Mr. Ascher continue to work the vein he has so auspiciously opened.

And dull with scowling clouds and fretful skies,
The little days pass onward to their bourne—
Life's shadowy landmarks, to our saddened eyes,
But vanished haze of morn!

The hours shrivel as we vainly try
To grasp their fruits within our feeble hold;
Their glow and bloom and beauty seem to die
In winter's piercing cold.

O lessening days that silently depart!
Leave us the broader faith and larger hope,
So that the scarred and patient human heart
May love with fuller scope:

Yield us the deeper trust in human truth,
Show us the purer sky above the haze,
So that the nobler visions of our youth
May light our devious ways:

Banish the frost of doubt that numbs the heart,
Broaden the narrowing limits of life's road;
So may your fleeting presence still impart
A lasting love for God.

THE DYING WARRIOR.

HELEN M. JOHNSTON.

A warrior lay, with a heaving breast,
On the field of the dying and dead;
His cheek was pale and his lips compressed,
And the fading light from the distant west
Shone over his gory bed.

The night came on, and the moon arose
With her soft and tremulous glow;
She shed her light o'er friends and o'er foes,
All sleeping together in dull repose
On the battle-field below.

The warrior gazed with a mournful sigh
On the blue and the star-spangled dome;
While tears shone bright in his sunken eye,
And his vivid thoughts like the lightning fly
To his childhood's distant home.

He thought of the mother who used to bend
O'er his couch, when in sorrow and pain—
Who to his complaints an ear would lend;
But alas! he knew that that dearest friend
Would never bend o'er him again.

He thought of the scenes where once he strayed
With his brothers in days of yore;
He thought of the stream, the peaceful glade,
The cottage that stood in the dark green shade,
With the vines around the door.

He thought, with a pang of dark despair,
'Twas the hour they all used to meet
With grateful hearts for the evening prayer;
He thought of the group that were gathered there;
He thought—of a vacant seat.

He knew that a fervent prayer would rise
For the loved and the long-absent one;
He knew that the tears would flow from their eyes,
And his father's voice would be choked with sighs,
As he prayed for his erring son.

He knew for him they would all implore
  A renewed and a sanctified heart;
That when the toils of this life were o'er
They all might embrace each other once more,
  Never, no never to part!

One trembling hand to his brow he pressed,
  And the tears of contrition he shed;
He implored for pardon, a home with the blest;
Then he wrapped his cloak round his gory breast,
  And the warrior's spirit fled!

SEEKING.

ANNIE L. WALKER.

Where dost Thou dwell,
Unknown, unseen, yet knowing, seeing all?
We find Thee not in hermit's lonely cell,
  Nor lofty palace-hall.

No more at eve
Thy form is with us on the dusty road;
The dead sleep on, though loving hearts may grieve
  The suffering bear their load.

Night closes round—
In the green forest-aisles no leaf is stirred;
So hushed, as if heaven's distant music sound
  Might even here be heard.

Through all we see,
Up to the azure roof with stars inwrought,
Through all Earth's temple, do we look for Thee;
Alas! we find Thee not.

Yet Thou art near;
Father! forgive our weak and failing sight;
Forgive, and make our darkness noonday clear
With thy celestial light.

Thy love has given
Faith's telescope, wherewith to gaze on Thee;
Aid us, that through it looking unto heaven,
Thy glory we may see.

WHAT DO WE LIVE FOR?*

JENNIE E. HAIGHT.

What do we live for?
Is labor so lowly,
Toil so ignoble, we shrink from its stain?
Think it not—labor
Is Godlike and holy;
He that is idle is living in vain.

---

*There is in this piece, as in nearly all Miss Haight's poetry, the utterance of an intensely earnest spirit, which rings out like the sound of a clarion, summoning all true hearts to arise and do battle for truth, right, and humanity. She writes like one who feels deeply the import of the great social questions of the age, and cherishes an ardent desire for the social and moral elevation of mankind. Her poetry has no aimless loitering, or flower-gathering by the way: it goes like an arrow to its mark, stirring the soul to noble deeds of patient endurance and unselfish heroism.

What do we live for?
Creation is groaning,
Her desolate places are yet to be built;
The voice of the years
Swells deeper the moaning,
As time rolls along the dark tide of guilt.

What do we live for?
The question is sounding
Low in the silence, and loud in the din,
And to each heart-ear,
With warm pulses bounding,
Answers come thronging, without and within.

What do we live for?
We live to be waging
Battle, unceasing, with indwelling sin;
We live to fight on,
In conflict engaging
Temptations without, and passions within.

What do we live for?
To sow, by all waters,
Fruit-bearing seeds of deeds for all years;
To toil in the ranks
With earth's sons and daughters,
Manfully striving with doubtings and fears.

Miss Haight is a teacher in an educational institution in the city of Montreal. For several years she has been an occasional contributor of short pieces to Canadian journals; and there is none of our young writers who has met with more favor, both from the public and press. She is one of the very few of whom we feel that they have written too little.

What do we live for?
We live not to rust out,
Slothfully standing aloof from the strife;
A thousand times better,
More noble, to wear out,
Battered and burned in the hot forge of life.

TO THE SEA.

JAMES M'CARROLL.

Unfathomable waste of winds and waves,
And stars that tuft the purple woof of night,
And pin it, shadowed down, amid thy depths—
How great art thou in all thy twofold strength!
Whether one vast unbroken sheet of calm,
Where the long finger of the lonely mast
Points through the azure solitude, to God!
Or whether, from out thy solemn slumbers roused,
Shaking thy dripping hide and awful crest,
Thou goest forth to meet the fierce typhoon
That, plumed with darkness, blurred with fire and flame,
Scatters thy fleets 'mid shoals and sunken rocks,
And leaves them like dead sea-fowl drifting there!

How great art thou!—at morn!—or noon!—or eve,
When through the crimson portals of the West
The huge, red furnace of the dying day
Pours out its lava o'er thy radiant floor,
Till thou art as the vestibule of heaven

Leading to the great llanos of the sun,
That carpets the dread space before His throne;
And till the earth clasped in thy glowing arms
In emerald splendor 's borne along its path,
And thou dost seem a giant ruby set
In the broad chasing of a thousand shores,
Where thou dost meet the sea shells and the sands,
A rim of golden dust, and pearl and rose.

"I AM NOT SAD."

JOHN READE.

I.

I am not sad; I have a hope that tells
Of joys that live beyond the things of earth,
That springs from little seeds of love, and dwells
Deep in the bosom where it had its birth.
And those who sowed the little seeds of love,
In the bright spring-time of life's fleeting year,
Still kindly watch the blossom from above,
And come to see their love's sweet fruit appear
EVER, or in the still of summer noons,
Or when the sun is smiling his adieu,
Or when the night-harp breathes its solemn tunes,
Or when the birds begin their mates to woo,
EVER, their hallowed presence lingers near,
Unseen but by my spirit's sleepless eye,
And gentle words fall on my soul's quick ear,
Loving and low as mother's lullaby:
I am not sad.

II.

I am not sad; though sorrows not a few
Have left their darksome trace upon my brow,
Still hopeful, I can life's rough way pursue,
And 'neath the load of duty meekly bow.
For sorrows are but ministers of God,
Sent to remind us of the home we seek;
The path of sorrow He before us trod,
Who taught the blind to see, the dumb to speak.
When storm-clouds gather o'er the placid sky,
The dull, foreboding drapery of gloom,
God's bow of beauty tells the anxious eye,
Man shall not perish by a watery doom.
So through the eye of faith afar I read
Bright promises amid the clouds of woe.
When God has promised, should I be afraid?
Should I be sad and weak and doubtful? No;
I am not sad.

III.

I am not sad; "man was not made to mourn,"
To drown in dreary wretchedness his years,
Though hate and wrong, and penury and scorn
Oft make this world indeed a "vale of tears."
Still Eden-flowers in earthly gardens grow,
Still man does deeds of mercy and of love,
And the dread curse that's written on his brow
Is half-effaced by blessings from above.
Have I to toil? God sends me cheerful light;
Have I to suffer? He can make me brave;
Am I sore tempted? He can keep me right;
Am I in danger? He can surely save;

Am I a wanderer? He has sent His Son,
To bring me weary, heavy-laden, HOME,
To worship THERE with angels round the throne,
And never from His presence more to roam:
I am not sad.

OLD HANNAH.

ALEXANDER M'LACHLAN.

'Tis Sabbath morn, and a holy balm
Drops down on the heart like dew,
And the sunbeams gleam,
Like a blessed dream,
Afar on the mountains blue.
Old Hannah's by her cottage door
In her faded widow's cap;
She is sitting alone
On the old grey stone,
With the Bible in her lap.

An oak is hanging o'er her head,
And the burn is wimpling by,
The primroses peep
From their sylvan keep,
And the lark is in the sky.
Beneath that shade her children played;
But they're all away with death!
And she sits alone
On the old grey stone,
To hear what the Spirit saith.

Her years are o'er three score and ten,
And her eyes are waxing dim,
But the page is bright
With a living light,
And her heart leaps up to Him
Who pours the mystic harmony
Which the soul can only hear;
She is not alone
On the old grey stone,
Though no earthly friend is near.

There's no one left to love her now;
But the eye that never sleeps
Looks on her in love
From the heavens above,
And with quiet joy she weeps.
She feels the balm of bliss is poured
In her worn heart's deepest rut;
And the widow lone
On the old grey stone,
Has a peace the world knows not.

DEATH OF CAPTAIN VICARS.

HARRIETT A. WILKINS.

There were sound of armies gathering
Unto the cannon's roll;
There were sounds of martial melody
Before Sebastopol.

Courage was mantling in the breast,
And fire in many an eye,
As Britain's gallant hosts moved on
To conquer or to die.

There were noble veterans in that train
Who boasted many a scar;
There was one who led his gallant band,
Young in those scenes of war;
Young, but how loved!—ah, many an eye
That saw him arming there
Was raised to bless him, as his voice
Broke through the misty air,
"This way, 97th!

"By the flags that o'er us wave,
All that makes the brave heart brave;
By the ties of home's sweet band,
Sheltered on our native land;
By the ashes of our sires—
By the light of Britain's fires—
This way, 97th!

"By the burning vows that rest
Deep within the patriot's breast;
By the bayonets that gleam
In the young moon's flickering beam;
Though we stand on danger's marge,
God will help us—up and charge!
This way, 97th!

"He will arm us for this fight,
On this strange, this fearful night.

Ere we route the treach'rous foe
Some of us may slumber low;
See that each is ready—then,
Fight and die like Christian men.
"This way, 97th!

"Forward! victory is ours,
Though we fall beneath yon towers:
England's glory is our crest—
England's colors wrap our breast—
Let the trenches witness bear
That the dauntless brave fell there;
This way, 97th!"

Fierce was the battle—wild the strife—
The ground beneath them rang;
Redan and Malakoff that night
Echoed the musket's clang;
Two thousand of the treach'rous host
Advanced 'neath that dark sky;
Two hundred of Victoria's men
Had met them at the cry,
"This way, 97th!"

They fought and conquered, but the voice
That led them bravely on,
The tone that cheered their lion-hearts
For evermore was gone.
Yet as the life-blood flowed apace,
He saw his victory won,
And once more shouted as he fell,
"Brethren, the foemen run!
This way, 97th!"

He died as many have gone down,
    Who bear the warrior's crest,
With a treasured name upon his lips,
    And a locket on his breast.
Oh, would ye learn how brave men fight;
    Go where the bravest lie!
And would ye learn how fond hearts love,
    And how true Christians die—
        "This way, 97th!"

Ye who beside him fought and won,
    Still may ye hear the sound
That from the watch, the camp, the war,
    Hath gone to holier ground;
The voice that failed on Russia's plain
    Awoke to sweeter song,
And still he whispers by your side,
    While beckoning on your throng,
        "This way, 97th!"

Oh, ye throughout our land, who gird
    The sword upon your side,
And stand prepared in danger's hour
    To rush in battle's tide,
Scorn not to seek the light he sought—
    Scorn not the path he trod,
Through woes to victory on earth,
    Then glory with his God.

UNDER THE SNOW.*

PAMELIA S. VINING.

Over the mountains, under the snow
Lieth a valley cold and low,
'Neath a white immovable pall,
Desolate, dreary, soulless all,
And soundless, save when the wintry blast
Sweeps with funeral music past.

Yet was that valley not always so,
For I trod its summer-paths long ago,
And I gathered flowers of fairest dyes
Where now the snow-drift heaviest lies,
And I drank from rills that with murmurous song
Wandered in golden light along
Through bowers, whose ever-fragrant air
Was heavy with perfume of flowrets fair—

---

* There is no Canadian poet whose poetry we have read, and re-read, with greater interest and delight than Miss Vining's. This piece is no ordinary production. It contains beautiful imagery; a sound and elevated philosophy of suffering; great depth and tenderness of feeling; and a rich exquisite rhythmic music, that lingers in "the chambers of the brain," like the memory of a speechless joy. The snow, that silently and sadly buries all the glory of summer beneath its icy shroud, is here taken, as the suggestive type of that wintry blight that sooner or later falls on every life, withering its brightest blossoms in hopeless decay. Shallcw and thoughtless hearts, blinded by the glare of frothy pleasures and sordid pursuits, may see no special beauty in such poetry; but readers of more delicate sensibility, whose bygone years are shaded by the memory of deep sorrow, will feel the influence of its uncommon beauty, tenderness, and truth. MISS VINING is a teacher in the Canadian Institute at Woodstock. We understand that she intends shortly publishing a volume of original poetry. We bespeak for it a favorable reception from the Canadian public.

Through cool green meadows, where all day long
The wild-bee droned his voluptuous song,
While over all shone the eye of Love
In the violet-tinted heavens above.

And through that valley ran veins of gold,
And the rivers o'er beds of amber rolled ;—
There were pearls in the white sands thickly sown,
And rocks that diamond-crusted shone ;—
All richest fruitage—all rarest flowers—
All sweetest music of summer bowers—
All sounds the softest—all sights most fair,
Made earth a Paradise everywhere.

* * * *

Over the mountains, under the snow
Lieth that valley cold and low,—
There came no slowly consuming blight,
But the snow swept silently down at night,
And when the morning looked forth again
The seal of silence was on the plain ;
And fount and forest, and bower and stream
Were hidden all from his pallid beam.

And there, deep-hidden under the snow,
Is buried the wealth of the long ago—
Pearls and diamonds—veins of gold,
Priceless treasures of worth untold,
Harps of wonderful sweetness stilled
While yet the air was with music filled—
Hands that stirred the resounding string
To melodies such as the angels sing—

Faces radiant with smile and tear
That bent enraptured the strains to hear—
And high calm foreheads, and earnest eyes,
That came and went beneath sunset skies.

There they are lying under the snow,
And the winds moan over them sad and low.
Pale still faces that smile no more,
Calm closed eyelids whose light is o'er,
Silent lips that will never again
Move to music's entrancing strain,
White hands folded o'er marble breasts,—
Each under the mantling snow-drift rests,
And the wind their requiem sounds o'er and o'er,
In the oft repeated 'no more—*no more.*'

'*No more—no more!*'—I shall ever hear
That funeral dirge in its moanings drear;
But I may not linger with faltering tread
Anear my treasures—anear my dead.
On through many a thorny maze,
Up slippery rocks, and through tangled ways,
Lieth my cloud-mantled path, afar
From that buried vale where my treasures are.

But there bursts a light through the heavy gloom,
From the sun-bright towers of my distant home;
Fainter the wail of the sad '*no more*'
Is heard as slowly I near that shore;
And sweet home-voices come soft and low,
Half-drowning that requiem's dirge-like flow.

I know it is Sorrow's baptism stern
That has given me thus for my home to yearn—
That has quickened my ear to the tender call
Which down from the jasper heights doth fall—
And lifted my soul from the songs of earth
To music of higher and holier birth,
Turning the tide of a yearning love
To the beautiful things that are found above;—
And I bless my Father, through blinding tears,
For the chastening love of departed years,—
For hiding my idols so low—*so low*—
Over the mountains,—under the snow.

SPRING.

J. J. PROCTER.

Light upon the wild-flowers dawning from on high!
Light upon the white clouds floating in the sky!
Light upon the green fields, light upon the rill!
Happy morn is breaking o'er each lofty hill.

Music in the rustling of the summer trees!
Music in the many tones that sweep along the breeze!
Music in the little birds that haunt the budding spray!
Winter's snows are melting—Spring is on its way.

Gladness in the mountains! gladness in the plains!
Gladness in all nature, bursting from her chains!
Gladness in the waters, rippling down their streams!
Heaven and earth rejoicing in the sun's bright beams.

Happy, happy spring-time! Happy age of youth!
Rich in aspirations, rich in love and truth!
Use it well, lest summer scorch ye with its sun,
And your budding beauties droop, ere yet begun.

THE GOOD MAN'S GRAVE.

FREDERICK WRIGHT.

E'en such is man—a shadow flies
Athwart the trembling moonlit skies,
Man heaves a breath, and lo! he dies;
        But not for aye!
His soul may yet triumphant rise,
        A brighter day!

Though like a flower of loveliest bloom,
That yields at morn its rich perfume,
And e'er the night hath met its doom
        The good man dies;
Yet sweetly from the loathsome tomb
        His actions rise!

The blessings of his kindly heart,
The balm his soothing words impart,
His life's example for a chart
        By which to steer,
From memory's eye cannot depart,
        Or disappear.

Most when we feel the aching void
Made by our blissful hopes destroyed,
And all our energies are cloyed
With gloom and care,
Could we more fitly be employed
Than musing there?

Beneath this resting-place we find
A fitting theme for musing mind
That is not to its errors blind;
But seeks to mend,
And leaving earthly cares behind,
See where they end.

The highest aim we self-impose,
The noblest height ambition knows,
The loftiest wing that ever rose
In flight sublime,
May end in disappointment's throes,
Perhaps in crime!

Not so, the even, steady race
Of him who, yielding wisdom place,
Adorned by humble pilgrim grace,
Keeps on the road,
And walks erect, with fearless pace,
To meet his God.

Though carking cares his path surround,
And sin should raise her rampant mound,
He bravely stands on battle ground,
Nor shrinks with fear:
Faith is the balm for every wound,
And refuge near.

His trust in God is firmly stayed;
God's love, his ready shield, displayed,
And strong in mercy, undismayed
He bids them come!
Nor dreads the countless hosts arrayed
'Twixt him and home!

THE ARCTIC INDIAN'S FAITH.

HON. T. D. M'GEE.

We worship the Spirit that walks unseen
Through our land of ice and snow:
We know not His face, we know not His place,
But His presence and power we know.

Does the Buffalo need the Pale-face word
To find his pathway far?
What guide has he to the hidden ford,
Or where the green pastures are?
Who teacheth the Moose that the hunter's gun
Is peering out of the shade?
Who teacheth the doe and the fawn to run
In the track the Moose has made?

Him do we follow, Him do we fear,
The Spirit of earth and sky;
Who hears with the *Wapiti's* eager ear
His poor red children's cry;

Whose whisper we note in every breeze
That stirs the birch canoe;
Who hangs the reindeer-moss on the trees
For the food of the *Caribou.*

That Spirit we worship who walks unseen
Through our land of ice and snow:
We know not His face, we know not His place,
But His presence and power we know.

SONG OF MARY MAGDALENE.

ALEXANDER M'LACHLAN.

Weep not, though the Saviour
   Has gone with the dead,
For the light and the glory
   Still halo his head;
The sighs and the sorrows,
   The stigmas, the stains:
The anguish is over,
   The glory remains.

Weep not for the Saviour:
   His sorrows are o'er,
And his love shall encircle
   Our hearts evermore;
The rainbow of promise!
   The star ever bright!
The compass to guide through
   The perilous night!

The light of the temple!
  The eye of the blind!
The food of the hungry!
  The friend ever kind!
The well in the desert!
  The shield from the blast!
The staff of the weary!
  The refuge at last!
The sun of our glory!
  The light of our eyes!
Weep not for the Saviour,
  For he shall arise.

VOICES OF THE DEATH-CHAMBER.

MRS. J. L. LEPROHON.

The night-lamp faintly gleameth
  Within my chamber still,
And the heavy shades of midnight
  Each gloomy angle fill;
And my worn and wearied watchers
  Scarce dare to move or weep,
For they think that I am buried
  In deep and quiet sleep.

But hush! what are those voices
  Rising on the midnight air;
Full of strange, celestial sweetness,
  Breathing love and hope and prayer!

Nearer still they grow and clearer;
  Ah! I hear now what they say—
To the kingdom of God's glory
  They are calling me away.

See! my gentle mother softly
  To my couch approaches now—
What can be the change she readeth
  Upon my pale, damp brow,
That she clasps her hands in anguish,
  Whose wild depths no words might say?
Perchance she has heard the voices
  That are calling me away.

The fond father of my children,
  The first sole love of my youth;
He the loving, gentle-hearted,
  So full of manly truth,
Is kneeling now beside me,
  Wildly praying me to stay:
'Tis hard, oh! hard to tell him,
  "They are calling me away!"

Oh! if earthly love could conquer
  The mighty power of death,
His love would stay the current
  Of my failing strength and breath;
And that voice whose loving fondness
  Has been e'er my earthly stay,
Could half tempt me from the voices
  That are calling me away.

Now, they bring my children to me,
  That loved and lovely band,
And with wistful awe-struck-faces
  Around my couch they stand,
And I strain each gentle darling
  To my heart with wailing cry,
And for the first time murmur,
  "Oh, my God, 'tis hard to die!"

But hark! those strains of heaven
  Sound louder in mine ear,
Whispering, "He, thy God, thy Father,
  Will guard those children dear"—
Louder yet they grow, now drowning
  All sounds of mortal birth;
In their wild triumphant sweetness
  Luring, bearing me from earth.

THE EMIGRANT'S FUNERAL.

REV. R. J. M'GEORGE.

Strange earth we sprinkle on the exile's clay,
  Mingled with flowers his childhood never knew;
Far sleeps he from that mountain-top so blue,
Shadowing the scene of his young boyhood's play.
But o'er his lonely trans-atlantic bed
  The ancient words of hopeful love are spoken;
  The solitude of these old pines is broken
With the same prayers once o'er his father said.

O precious Liturgy! that thus canst bring
Such sweet associations to the soul,
That though between us and our homes seas roll,
We oft in thee forget our wanderings,
And in a holy day-dream tread once more,
The fresh green valleys of our native shore.

"MY SOUL IS HEAVY."

JOHN READE.

My soul is heavy with the chain
That drags me down to earth; in vain
I try to free me from its pain.

And yet I ask not wealth or fame,
I ask not power nor titled name,—
Only my Saviour's love I claim.

I fain would fix my wandering eye
Upon my treasure in the sky,
Bought by His death on Calvary.

But I am weak; my soul's best prayer
To Heaven, falls earthward, as it were
Afraid of gaining access *there*.

Earthward, where my soul's hopes are not;
Where I have but a pilgrim's lot:
Why is my Father's home forgot?

Earth's fairest scenes must pass away,
Man's mightiest monuments decay,
And the poor traveller may not stay.

O Comforter Divine, appear,
Impart the love that knows not fear,
And let me feel Thee ever near.

Then shall my soul, from earthly things
Set free, soar up on tireless wings,
To where God's choir for ever sings.

I COME TO THE WELL.

WILLIAM WYE SMITH.

I come to the well, but its water
  Never quenches the thirsting within,—
I bathe in the sunlight of morning,
  When the hymns of creation begin,—
And still there is something of sorrow,
  Because there is something of sin.

There is rapture and gladness and glory
  Around me in Nature I see,
And my heart whispers sadly the story
  That the darkness and doubt is in me;
That God and his works are all holy,
  And the sadness and sin is in me!

But I know that *above* there are blossoms
  As fair as were Eden's at first;
And the tree with the sweet leaves of healing,
  And waters for quenching of thirst;
And grief is forgot in the glory,
  And murmuring never rehearsed!

GO, DREAM NO MORE.

PAMELIA S. VINING.

Go, dream no more of a sun-bright sky
  With never a cloud to dim!
Thou hast seen the storm in its robes of night,
Thou hast felt the rush of the whirlwind's might,
Thou hast shrunk from the lightning's arrowy flight,
  When the Spirit of Storms went by!

Go, dream no more of a crystal sea
  Where never a tempest sweeps!
For thy riven bark on a surf-beat shore,
Where the wild winds shriek and the billows roar,
A shattered wreck to be launched no more,
  Will mock at thy dream and thee!

Go, dream no more of a fadeless flower
  With never a cankering blight!
For the queenliest rose in thy garden-bed,
The pride of the morn, ere the noon is fled,
With the worm at its heart, withers cold and dead
  In the Spoiler's fearful power!

Go, dream no more! for the cloud will rise,
  And the tempest will sweep the sea;
Yet grieve not thou, for beyond the strife,
The storm, and the gloom with which earth is rife,
Gleam out the light of immortal life,
  And the glow of unchanging skies!

I SHALL DEPART.

HELEN M. JOHNSON.

When the flowers of Summer die,
When the birds of Summer fly,
When the winds of Autumn sigh,
    I shall depart!

When the mourning earth receives
Last of all the faded leaves,
When the wailing forest grieves,
    I shall depart!

When are garnered grain and fruit,
When all insect life is mute,
I shall drop my broken lute,
    I shall depart!

When the fields are brown and bare,
Nothing left that 's good or fair,
And the hoar-frost gathers there,
    I shall depart!

Not with you, oh! songsters, no!
To no Southern clime I go,
By a way none living know
I shall depart!

Many aching hearts may yearn,
Many lamps till midnight burn,
But I never shall return
When I depart!

Trembling, fearing, sorely tried,
Waiting for the ebbing tide,
Who, oh! who will be my guide,
When I depart?

Once the river cold and black
Rolled its waves affrighted back—
I shall see a shining track,
When I depart!

There my God and Saviour passed,
He will guide me to the last;
Clinging to his merits fast,
I shall depart!

EVER WITH THEE.

ANNIE L. WALKER.

No more in darkness, trials, and temptations,
No more a waif on trouble's billowy sea,
How sweet will be the day of my abiding
Ever with Thee!

Bright after darkness shines the summer morning,
Bright is the sunshine when the tempests flee;
But brighter far the home where dwell thy chosen
Ever with Thee.

Dear are the hours when those we love are near us;
Dear, but how transient must their brightness be!
That one glad day will know no sadder morrow
Ever with Thee.

Love will be there: methinks all other glories
Nothing to those enraptured souls will be,
Filled with the transport of that one assurance,
Ever with Thee.

But long may be the way that we must travel,
And many a dark'ning storm we yet may see,
Dread sorrows may o'erwhelm us ere we're sheltered
Ever with Thee.

Not so: thy hand, extended through the darkness,
Leadeth us on the way we cannot see,
And, clasping that, e'en here we walk in safety
Ever with Thee.

DEATH OF THE PAUPER CHILD.*

MRS. J. L. LEPROHON.

Hush, mourning mother, wan and pale!
No sobs, no grieving now:
No burning tears must thou let fall
Upon that cold, still brow;
No look of anguish cast above,
Nor smite thine aching breast,
But clasp thine hands, and thank thy God
Thy darling is at rest.

Close down those dark-fringed snowy lids
Over the violet eyes,
Nor heed their liquid light was clear
As that of summer skies.
Is it not bliss to know whate'er
Thy future griefs and fears,
They will be never dimmed like thine
By sorrow's scalding tears!

---

* We remember MRS. LEPROHON (R. E. M.), as an interesting contributor to the "Literary Garland" of former days. She has been for many years a favourite contributor in prose and verse to Canadian and American periodicals. Her poetry is marked by simplicity and gracefulness of style, strong domestic and human sympathies, and high moral sentiment. The pieces in this volume, "*The Death of the Pauper Child,*" and "*Given and Taken,*" unveil deep womanly tenderness and truth. Her achievements in prose-fiction have won her higher distinction, and made her still more extensively known than her poetry. Her poems have never, we believe, been published in book form. Several of her friends think it is due to herself and to the public, to collect her fugitive pieces, and present them in a form suitable for permanent preservation.

Enfold the tiny fingers fair,
From which life's warmth has fled,
Forever freed from wearing toil—
The strife for daily bread:
Compose the softly moulded limbs,
The little waxen feet,
Spared way-side journeys long and rough,
Spared many a weary beat.

Draw close around the lifeless form,
The shreds of raiment torn,
Her only birth-right—just such rags
As thou for years hast worn;
Her earthly dower the bitter crust,
She might from pity crave,
Moistened by tears—then, final gift,
A pauper's lowly grave.

Now raise thy spirit's gaze above!
Seest thou yon angel fair,
With flowing robes, and starry crown
Gemming her golden hair?
Changed, glorified in every trait,
Still in that beauty mild,
O! mourning mother, thou dost know
Thine own, thy late lost child.

Wrapped in heaven's entrancing bliss,
Veiled in its golden glow,
Still thinks she of the lonely heart
Left on this earth below.

Courage!—not long thy weary steps
O'er barren wastes shall roam;
Thy darling prays the Father now
To quickly call thee HOME.

DREAMS OF THE DEAD.*

J. J. PROCTER.

I.

Oh let me dream for awhile
    Under the winter sky;
Dream of the light of a vanished smile,
    And the hope of a day gone by;
Dream of a lovely face,
    And the grace of a lovely head,
And the form that I clasped in a fond embrace—
    Let me dream for awhile of the dead.

Dead! can it be I am here
    Whispering this to my heart?
Dead! and I have not one welcome tear
    To soften the inward smart!
Dead! and I cannot pray,
    For I think of my love that is gone,
And the hope that was withered in one short day,
    Has blasted my heart to stone.

---

* "*The Voices of the Night, and other poems,*" by J. J. PROCTER, was published by Mr. Lovell of Montreal, in 1861. Mr. Procter's poetry evinces a cultivated taste, and an affluence of fancy that at times reminds one of Shelley or of Tennyson. There is, however, a monotony of both style and feeling, pervading a large portion of the book, which detracts something from its interest and merit. The poet's soul is steeped in sorrow; and, though never commonplace, this shadow of sorrow darkens all subjects with an intense and morbid melancholy, that becomes at length oppressive. But in spite of these defects, this volume displays unmistakable poetic feeling and power. We understand that, as yet, it has had a very limited circulation.

What have I left but to dream
    Of my love that is laid in her rest,
To live as I lived, for my life's years seem
    But an empty dream at the best!
Everything round is still,
    And white as a new-made shroud,
From the snow-clad lea to the pines on the hill,
    And the fleecy veil of the cloud.

Here on the snow I lie
    Seeking a balm for care,
Looking up to the blank of the sky,
    And the blue of the fathomless air.
Hark! how the chill winds wail,
    And shiver and moan in their flight;
What a depth of woe in the sorrowful tale
    They tell in the ear of night!

What is it that makes them sad?
    Do they miss the grace of the flowers,
And sigh for the time when their breath was glad
    With the sweets of the summer hours?
Ye do well, chill winds, to rave,
    For the day of your brides has fled,
The earth lies heavy and cold on their grave,
    They are dead—and she too is dead!

II.

Swoon into sleep, O night,
    For the air is heavy and still,
And the shimmering glance of the moonbeam's light
    Comes down like a deadly chill.

Oh sink, pale orb, in the west;
Sink down in the west till I see
Her who lies long in her last long rest,
Waiting alone for me.

Last eve, in my dreams, the veil
Of the frost-bound earth was gone,
And I saw her lying all cold and pale
Like an angel fashioned in stone.
The glance that could give me life
Was asleep in the downcast eye;
But the rose of thy lips, O love, O wife,
Was bright with a smile from on high.

How sweet was her calm repose
And the smile that told of Heaven!
No passion, no tear, no fears, no woes,
But the bliss of sin forgiven.
I heard the flakes of the snow
Fall soft through the winter air,
And the foul worm crawl from his couch below,
But I knew that her God was there.

There, in the silent grave,
Whence everything else had fled,
Was the presence of Him who had died to save,
Watching the sleep of the dead.
There was the Lord of Hosts
Guarding the rest of my sweet,
And Death, with his conqueror's pride and boasts,
Crouched down at her Father's feet.

Let me dream thus again
    Seeing her under the sward:
What better relief for my heavy pain,
    Than to know her there with her Lord?
Farewell for a time, dear love:
    Methinks I have much to learn;
For a strange light moves in the heavens above,
    And a voice that bids me return.

SONG OF CONFIDENCE.*

HARRIETT ANNIE WILKINS.

"I will trust, and not be afraid."—Bible.

My path is in the wilderness,
    My way is in the desert wild,
And dreary wastes and loneliness
    Mingle with rocks, in terror piled;
Yet One has promised he will guide
    To lands whose treasures never rust;
I have upon his strength relied—
    Can He sustain me? "I will trust!"

My path is through the waters cold,
    And billows rise on every side;
I hear the noise where breakers rolled,
    I feel their overpowering tide:

---

* From THE ACACIA, by HARRIET ANNIE. A new and enlarged edition of this volume has been just issued from the press. MISS WILKINS of Hamilton has been favourably known for many years as a contributor of verse to Canadian journals. She is a spirited and vigorous writer, distinguished by strong patriotic and martial feeling; and by a deeply religious spirit, which constantly recognizes scriptural piety as the true source of strength and consolation.

A hand is on the flowing mane
  Of ocean's charger—stay it must;
One holds the breakers' bridle-rein,
  And can He curb them? "I will trust!"

The noon-tide sun is high in heaven,
  Its rays are bending o'er my brow;
No streamlet 'mid this sand is given,
  No green oasis near me now:
Nearer it comes—the siroc storm,
  Scorching and burning is its dust;
Yet I saw one in human form,
  The Good Physician—"I will trust!"

The evening cometh; I would rest,
  And in forgetfulness repose,
But rain-drops stream upon my breast,
  Forbidding my worn eyes to close;
Yet 'mid the tempest's hollow moan,
  The lightning's glare, the whirlwind's gust,
I surely heard a soft low tone—
  I know its whisper—"I will trust!"

As on my weary way I passed,
  A bright star lit my midnight sky;
I prized its beauty—but a blast
  With heavy clouds went sweeping by:
A voice came murmuring from above,
  "Mourner, yield not to sad mistrust;
Again shall gleam that star of love,
  Fond and for ever;" "I will trust!"

Oh! can it be there waits on high
  A mansion now prepared for me?
And can I bear each weary sigh
  Until those golden gates I see?
Can He who loves preserve from harm,
  Re-animate my mould'ring dust,
Fold me within his shelt'ring arms,
  Happy for ever? "I will trust!"

INFINITE.

ALEXANDER M'LACHLAN.

Unbar the gates of eye and ear—
Lo! what a wondrous world is here,
Marvels, on marvels, still appear
                    Infinite!

Great Mother from whose breast we're fed!
With thy green mantle round thee spread,
The blue vault hanging o'er thy head
                    Infinite!

Why wert thou into being brought?
How were thy forms of beauty wrought?
Thou great upheaving of a thought
                    Infinite!

Which scooped the vales where dew distils,
Which led the courses of the rills,
And fixed the everlasting hills
                    Infinite!

Which called from darkness bright-ey'd day,
Baptized it with a heavenly ray,
And sent it on its endless way
Infinite!

Ye waves which lash the hoary steep,
Ye mighty minds with boundless sweep,
Great coursers of the trackless deep
Infinite!

And you ye streamlets on your way,
Though laughing all the summer's day
Ye only sing, ye only say
Infinite!

Sweet linnet singing on the lea!
Wild lark in heaven's wide azure sea!
The burden of your strain's to me
Infinite!

Lov'd violets 'neath my feet that lie,
Sweet harebells, can ye tell me why
Your beauty only makes me sigh
Infinite!

Thou wild rose blushing on the tree,
Ye daisies laughing on the lea,
Sweet flowers, your message is to me
Infinite!

This dust's to spirit strangely wed,
'Tis haunted ground on which we tread,
The living stranger than the dead
Infinite!

A presence fills the earth and air,
Hands help us when we're not aware,
And eyes look on us everywhere
Infinite!

Earth, ocean, air, heaven's azure sea!
O ye have always been to me
A marvel and a mystery
Infinite!

Who'll take the measure or the bound?
No line of ours can ever sound
The fathomless, the great profound
Infinite!

O! could I but from self get free,
The spirit then might speak thro' me
Of all this deep, unfathom'd sea
Infinite!

UNUTTERABLE THOUGHTS.*

JOHN READE.

......Quis prodere tanta relatu
... ..possit?
—CLAUDIAN.

There is a voice that never stirs the lips,—
Felt, but not heard; that vibrates through the soul,—
A solemn music; but no human speech
Can give that music to the ambient air.

---

*MR. READE has been for several years a poetic contributor to the Montreal press. His poetry contains true poetic feeling, and is replete with promise. He at present resides at Mascouche, C.E.

The noblest poem poet ever wrote;
The brightest picture artist ever drew;
The loftiest music lyrist ever sung;
The gentlest accents woman ever spoke,—
Are paraphrases of a *felt original*,
That lip, or pen, or pencil, cannot show
Unto the seeing eye or listening ear.
The thoughts we *utter* are but half themselves;
The poet knows this well. The artist knows
His hands bear not the burden of his thoughts
Upon the canvas. The musician knows
His soul must ever perish on his lips.
Oh, hast thou ever loved? Thou, too, canst tell
How little of thy love the air can bring
Unto the ear of her thou lov'st so well.
Nay, even the eye,—"the window of the soul,"—
Though it may shed a light a little way,
Gives but a glimpse of that which burns within.

The sweet, unconscious tenderness of flowers;
The boundless awe of star-encircled night;
The tear that trickles down an old man's cheek;
Ocean's loud pulse, that makes our own beat high;
The vocal throb of a great multitude;
The pause when you have heard and said, "Farewell!"
And feel the pressure of a hand that's gone;
The thought that you have wronged your truest friend,
When he is sleeping in the arms of Death;
The silent, fathomless anguish that engulfs
Him that has found the precious power to love,
And sees that *all* he loves is torn from him;
His dying moments who is void of hope;

Jezebel; Nero; Judas; any one
Of all the hideous things that crawled through life
In human form;—what mortal could express
All that he feels in one or all of *these*,
Giving the very image of his thought?

Life, Death, Hell, Judgment, Resurrection, God;—
Who can express *their* meaning? Who can bound
Awe that is infinite in finite words?

Thus, much of us must ever be concealed—
Spite of the high ambition to be born
Of what is noblest in us—till His breath
Who woke the morning-stars to sing their songs,
Awakes our souls to fuller utterance.

THE COMING YEAR.

JOHN F. M'DONNELL.

I do not weep for the bygone days,
Though they haunt my brain with their thrilling lays;
I do not yearn for the hours that are o'er,
Though I treasure their sweets in Memory's store;
Their weird perfume, like the winds of Spring—
Their hues as bright as a seraph's wing;
And their beams that play round each youthful thought,
Like a sunset glow by the mountains caught:
But why should I welcome the coming year,
When I know not yet if it brings good cheer?

The bygone year was a friend to me,
With its hours of pleasure light and free;
Its summer days, and its autumn eves,
And the spells that cling to its withered leaves;
Though its bloom soon fled, and its youth is lost,—
'Twas a dream of rest for the tempest-tossed;
Its fruits still cluster round Memory's vine,
And its wreaths through the dimness of Age shall shine:
Then why should I welcome the coming year,
When I know not yet if it brings good cheer?

There were smiles and tears in the shadowy Past,
But the gates of the Future are closed and fast.
Though clouds may have frowned on my pathway of old,
There were rainbow gleams on their sable fold;
The sunshine came when the waves were still,
And the May-day smiled after winter's chill.
I strive to gaze on the unknown shore,
But the veil of the Mystic hangs before!
Then why should I welcome the coming year,
When I know not yet if it brings good cheer?

There may be Peace in the unseen land,
And bowers of palm on its golden sand,
And flowers that blend with the morning breeze—
And isles of beauty on waveless seas;
Or it may be a region of death and gloom,
With a cypress grove and a gaping tomb;
And a clime like the frozen Norland hills,
Where the spirit sinks and the bosom chills:
Then why should I welcome the coming year,
When I know not yet if it brings good cheer?

The festal lights from the casements shine,
And the goblets are filled with the choicest wine;
For Mirth is the queen of the joyous throng,
With the laughter gay, and the ringing song;
The low fond whisper of Love and Truth,
And the grasp of Friendship and manly Youth;
But why do ye rush to the arms of the new,
When the kind old friend was so good and true—
Why welcome ye thus the coming year,
When ye know not yet if it brings good cheer?

THE SECOND ADVENT.

ANNIE L. WALKER.

In the hush of the silent midnight
Shall the cry of His coming be?
When the day of the Lord's appearing
Shall flash over earth and sea?

Shall it be at the morning's awaking,
And the beams of the golden sun
Grow pale and be quenched for ever,
When his journey is just begun?

We know not, we dream not, the hour;
But we know that the time must be
When earth, with its clouds and shadows,
Will shrink, and tremble, and flee;

---

* From "Leaves from the Backwoowds," published anonymously in 1861. This volume was favourably received by the press, and a second edition was issued, which, however, has had a very limited sale. It contains a number of pieces of much excellence, with some that are of a more feeble and commonplace character.

Will shrink to the deepest centre,
And render before his throne,
The Jewels the Lord will gather,
The gems that He calls his own.

Then, bright in heaven's noonday splendour,
And robed like the dazzling snow,
The saints to their many mansions,
The chosen and blest, shall go.

And songs of angelic gladness
Be borne on celestial air
To welcome the mighty gathering,
The throng, that shall enter there.

And, oh! in that awful parting,
That day of unchanging doom,
When earth shall give up her millions,
And empty her every tomb,

May we find in the Judge a Saviour,
A Friend, whom we know and love,
And be bidden by him to enter
The courts of his house above.

VOICES OF THE PAST.

E. H. DEWART.

The last faint gleam of Evening's golden light
Has softly died away: with noiseless hand
The Autumn twilight-shades enshroud from sight
Both sea and land.

In the hushed stillness of the darkened air,—
Like lonely echoes of the surging main,—
The Voices of the Past, with music rare,
Float through my brain.

Their mournful tones enchant my listening ear
Like spirit songs. They throng my soul unsought,
Rich with the hoarded gold of vanished years,
And pearls of thought.

Like winds and waves that swiftly, wildly sweep,
Freighted with treasures from some far-off clime,
They bear rich argosies across the deep,
Dark sea of time.

They tell of courtly pomp, and regal power
And fame, which now in dark oblivion lie,—
Of queenly beauty, fair as fairest flower,
Which bloomed to die;—

Of battles fought and bloody victories won,
For selfish lust of power and hollow fame,—
Of falsehood, tyranny, and crimes which none
Can calmly name;—

Of love, as changeless as the stars of heaven,—
Of joy that flashed,—like lightning o'er the deep,—
Leaving the soul in rayless tempests driven
To watch and weep;—

Of sunless paths where Doubt and Darkness lower,—
Of Superstition's black and ruthless reign,—
Of hero-faith, which gave the god-like power
To smile at pain;—

Of morn, unveiling truths long vainly sought,
Beaming refulgent o'er the weary night
Of years, gilding the hills and vales of thought
With holy light;—

Of Freedom battling with immortal might,
Baffled and crushed in vain, victorious still,—
Of kingly hearts, who still maintained the right
With iron will;—

Of Poet-souls whose grand immortal lays
Float over fallen thrones and royal names;
And some, who sang in sorrow all their days,
Oblivion claims;—

And ardent minds whose years of life were spent
Yearning for light, for truth, and spirit-rest;
But sought them not from God, and died at length,
Sad and unblest.

From thy dark bosom, unrelenting Past!
These whispers of the buried years are borne,—
Mysterious sunless sea! though deep and vast,
Lifeless and lorn!

No stormy winds disturb thy waveless breast,—
No starry skies dispel thine ebon gloom,—
All beauteous things, whose light and love have blessed,
There find a tomb.

Life, like a river from the future, sweeps
Along its shores with melody sublime,
Bearing forever to those silent deeps
The wrecks of time.

The wrecks of ardent love, of power and pride,—
Of hope, that vainly battled with despair,—
Of life, that sparkled like a mountain tide,—
Lie buried there.

Mysterious, grand, and melancholy Past!
Empire of death, oblivion, and decay!
Darkness shall veil thy depths, until the last
Great judgment day.

Till then thou holdest in thine iron hand
Records to which immortal fate is given,
Deeds that shall rise and shine at God's command,
As stars of heaven.

Unearthly Messengers, your tones remind
Of blighted blossoms of my wasted years,
Of broken vows and baffled hopes, which blind
With bitter tears.

And yet, these whispered notes of dirge-like tone
My sad and doubting heart with hope inspire,
For brighter burns, as time has onward flown,
Truth's beacon fire.

All earth-born glory dies and is forgot,
But all that Heaven's immortal founts supply,—
Truth, holy love, kind deeds, and noble thought,
Shall never die.

"AT EVENING TIME IT SHALL BE LIGHT."

J. E. HAIGHT.

O blessed light,
Infinite and supernal,
Gilding life's close with beams of radiance bright!
O blessed promise,
Breathed from lips eternal,
"At evening time it shall be light!"

In this I rest,
And dread no dark to-morrow,
Breaking in gloom upon a darker night;
Henceforth I walk
Beneath no cloud of sorrow,—
"At evening time it shall be light."

No more shall death,
Like some deep-shaded curtain,
Shut darkly down upon my wondering sight;
No longer shall I grope
My way through life, uncertain,—
"At evening time it shall be light."

I see the years
Glide on, with measured tread, unweeping—
I gaze, alike unmoved, on bloom or blight;
For still the promise sure,
My covenant-God is keeping,
"At evening time it shall be light."

I know the earth
Hath but a painful story;
That *now*, wrong triumphs o'er the true and right;—
But soon, for her,
This gloom shall change to glory!
" At evening time it shall be light."

Earth's evening time
Draws on, 'mid scenes of passing wonder,
Each day the powers of darkness gather might;
But God still reigns,
And we this precious truth may ponder,—
" At evening time it shall be light."

Earth groans in pain
And anguish for the new creation,
She counts each moment of her lingering night,—
Waiting the promise,
Long-delayed, of her salvation,—
" At evening time it shall be light."

I, too, look onward
To the evening time with hopeful spirit,
Its scenes of grandeur soon will greet my sight;
I know for me,
That, trusting in my Saviour's merit,
" At evening time it shall be light."

Oh! hasten Lord,
The coming of that blessed morrow,
Whose noonday radiance shall not wane to night;
That long-expected day,
When, darkened by no cloud of sin or sorrow,
" At evening time it shall be light."

National and Descriptive.

THE FINE OLD WOODS.

CHARLES SANGSTER.

Oh! come come away to the grave Old Woods,
Ere the skies are tinged with light,
Ere the slumbering leaves of the gloomy trees
Have shook off the mists of Night;
Ere the birds are up,
Or the floweret's cup
Is drained of its freshning dew,
Or the bubbing rill,
Kissing the hill,
Breaks on the distant view;
Oh ! such is the hour
To feel the power
Of the quiet, grave Old Woods!
Then, while sluggards dream
Of some dismal theme,
Let us stroll,
With prayerful soul,
Through the depths of the grave Old Woods.

Oh! come, come away to the bright Old Woods,
As the sun ascends the skies,
While the birdlings sing their morning hymns,
And each leaf in the grove replies;
When the golden-zoned bee
Flies from flower to tree,

Seeking sweets for its honeyed cell,
And the voice of Praise
Sounds its varied lays,
From the depth of each quiet dell:
Oh! such is the hour
To feel the power
Of the magic, bright Old Woods!
Then, while sluggards dream,
Of some trifling theme,
Let us stroll.
With studious soul,
Through the depths of the bright Old Woods.

Oh! come, come away to the mild Old Woods,
At the Evening's stilly hour,
Ere the maiden lists for her lover's steps,
By the verge of the vine-clad bower;
When all nature feels
The change that steals
So calmly o'er hill and dale,
And the breezes range
Weirdly strange,
With a low, delicious wail;
This, too, is the hour
To feel the power
Of the silent, mild Old Woods!
Then, while dullards dream
Of some fruitless theme,
We will stroll
With thankful soul,
Through the depths of the mild Old Woods.

Oh! come, come away to the calm Old Woods,
When the skies with stars are bright,
And the mild Moon moves in serenity,
The eye of the solemn night.
Not a sound is heard,
Save the leaflet stirred
By the zephyr that passes by,
And thought roams free
In its majesty,
And the soul seeks its kindred sky:
This, this is the hour
To test the power
Of the eloquent, calm Old Woods!
While the thoughtless dream
Of some baseless theme,
Here we can stroll,
With exalted soul,
Through the eloquent, calm Old Woods.

OUR NATIVE LAND.*

HELEN M. JOHNSON.

What land more beautiful than ours?
What other land more blest?
The South with all its wealth of flowers?
The prairies of the West?

---

* This spirited lyric is alike creditable to the talents, patriotism, and independence of its author. Its loyalty is an intelligent attachment, free from blind prejudice and crouching adulation. MISS JOHNSON'S poetry is characterized by unaffected simplicity, genuine sensibility, often tinged by sadness, a deep sense of the insuffi-

O no! there's not a fairer land
Beneath heaven's azure dome—
Where Peace holds Plenty by the hand,
And Freedom finds a home.

---

ciency of earthly good, and ardent aspirations after the things that are unseen and eternal. She was a native of Lower Canada; and died at Magog, C. E., in March, 1863, after a long and painful illness, in the 29th year of her age. The love of poetry, which early developed itself, in spite of circumstances the most unpropitious, proved a perennial source of solace and joy, to a life distinguished by more than an ordinary share of pain and suffering. In 1856, a small volume of her poems was published in Boston, U.S., which, although the edition is now exhausted, never circulated extensively in Canada. Though not free from the common faults of youthful authorship, this volume presented unmistakable evidence of a genuine gift of song. She continued from that time till the period of her death to contribute occasional pieces, for publication in the *Sherbrooke Gazette,* and other journals. Her unpublished poems, from which most of the selections in this work are taken, exhibit a more cultivated taste, and finished style, than we find in her published volume. Many of the pieces, among her unpublished remains, were evidently written under the influence of suffering, with the shadow of death gradually darkening her life. The pieces in this volume, "*I shall depart,*" "*To a Dandelion,*" and "*Good Night,*" illustrate this. She died in triumphant hope of immortality. The following lines, written with a pencil in her French testament, a few days before she died, give evidence of the clearness of her intellect, and the strength of her faith, as she approached "the river cold and black." They were the last she ever wrote.

Jesus, I know thou art the living Word!
Each blessed promise to myself I take;
I would not doubt, if I had only heard
This—this alone—"I NEVER WILL FORSAKE!"

I have no fear—the sting of death is sin,
And Christ removed it when He died for me:
Washed in his blood, my robe without, within,
Has not a stain that God himself can see.

Wrapped in the Saviour's arms I sweetly lie;
Far, far behind I hear the breakers roar;—
I *have* been dying—but I cease to die,
My rest begins—rejoice for evermore!

The slave who but her name hath heard,
  Repeats it day and night;—
And envies every little bird
  That takes its northward flight!

As to the Polar star they turn
  Who brave a pathless sea,—
So the oppressed in secret yearn,
  Dear native land for thee!

How many loving memories throng
  Round Britain's stormy coast!
Renowned in story and in song,
  Her glory is our boast!

With loyal hearts we still abide
  Beneath her sheltering wing;—
While with true patriot love and pride
  To Canada we cling!

We wear no haughty tyrant's chain,—
  We bend no servile knee,
When to the mistress of the main
  We pledge our fealty!

She binds us with the cords of love,—
  All others we disown;
The rights we owe to God above,
  We yield to him alone.

May He our future course direct
  By his unerring hand;
Our laws and liberties protect,
  And bless our native land!

JACQUES CARTIER.*

HON. T. D. M'GEE.

In the sea-port of Saint Malo 'twas a smiling morn in May,
When the Commodore Jacques Cartier to the westward sailed away;
In the crowded old Cathedral all the town were on their knees
For the safe return of kinsmen from the undiscovered seas;
And every autumn blast that swept o'er pinnacle and pier
Filled manly hearts with sorrow, and gentle hearts with fear.

A year passed o'er Saint Malo—again came round the day
When the Commodore Jacques Cartier to the westward sailed away;
But no tidings from the absent had come the way they went,
And tearful were the vigils that many a maiden spent;
And manly hearts were filled with gloom, and gentle hearts with
    fear,
When no tidings came from Cartier at the closing of the year.

But the earth is as the Future, it hath its hidden side,
And the Captain of Saint Malo was rejoicing in his pride
In the forests of the North—while his townsmen mourned his loss,
He was rearing on Mount-Royal the *fleur-de-lis* and cross;
And when two months were over and added to the year,
Saint Malo hailed him home again, cheer answering to cheer.

He told them of a region, hard, iron-bound and cold,
Nor seas of pearl abounded, nor mines of shining gold,

*MR. McGEE is better known to the Canadian public as an orator, a historian, and a politician, than as a poet. Though his poetry as a whole is scarcely equal to what his literary reputation in other departments might lead us to expect, yet many of the pieces in the "CANADIAN BALLADS" have the true ballad spirit and ring.

Where the wind from Thulè freezes the word upon the lip,
And the ice in spring comes sailing athwart the early ship;
He told them of the frozen scene until they thrill'd with fear,
And piled fresh fuel on the hearth to make them better cheer.

But when he chang'd the strain—he told how soon is cast
In early Spring the fetters that hold the waters fast;
How the Winter causeway broken is drifted out to sea,
And the rills and rivers sing with pride the anthem of the free;
How the magic wand of Summer clad the landscape to his eyes,
Like the dry bones of the just, when they wake in Paradise.

He told them of the Algonquin braves—the hunters of the wild,
Of how the Indian mother in the forest rocks her child;
Of how, poor souls, they fancy in every living thing
A spirit good or evil, that claims their worshipping;
Of how they brought their sick and maim'd for him to breathe upon,
And of the wonders wrought for them thro' the Gospel of St. John.

He told them of the river, whose mighty current gave
Its freshness for a hundred leagues to ocean's briny wave;
He told them of the glorious scene presented to his sight,
What time he reared the cross and crown on Hochelaga's height,
And of the fortress cliff that keeps of Canada the key,
And they welcomed back Jacques Cartier from his perils over sea.

THE DYING SUMMER.

ANNIE L. WALKER.

Gently, sadly, the summer is dying—
    Under the shivering, trembling boughs,
With a low soft moan, the breeze is flying—

The breeze, that was once so fresh and sweet,
Is passing as swift as Time's hurrying feet,
And where the withered roses are lying,
The beautiful summer is surely dying.

Gently, sadly, the waves are sighing,
    The leaves are mourning that they must fall;
And the plaintive waters keep replying,
They miss the light that has decked them long;
They have caught the last bird's farewell song;
And lowly they murmur, from day to day,
" The beautiful summer is passing away."

Gently, sadly, the moon reclining
    High on her throne of azure and gold,
With wan clear light, o'er the world is shining:
Wherever she turns there are tear-drops shed,
They will gleam, till the chilly morn is breaking,
And the flowers with their last pale smiles are waking.

Wildly, sadly, the night wind swelling,
    Chants a measure weird and strange,
Hark ! of the coming storm he is telling,
And the trembling life, that was almost gone,
Flickers and shrinks at the dreaded tone,
And scarcely lingers where, lowly lying,
The tender and beautiful summer is dying.

A CANADIAN SUMMER'S-NIGHT.*

(*With special emendations, by the author, for the present work.*)

E. J. CHAPMAN.

I.

The purple shadows dreamingly
Upon the dreaming waters lie,
And darken with the darkening sky.

Calmly across the lake we float,
I and thou, my little boat—
The lake, with its grey mist-capote.

We lost the moon an hour ago:
We saw it dip, and downward go,
Whilst all the west was still a-glow.

But in those blue depths, moon-forsaken,
A planet pale its place hath taken;
And one by one the stars awaken.

---

* We feel assured that our readers will agree with us, that there is a peculiar charm in this tranquil and picturesque description of "A Canadian Summer's Night," so rich with Canadian imagery and associations. There is a vein of quiet, tender feeling running through the poem, which, like a golden thread on which these images and incidents are strung, gives unity to the whole; while the intense sympathy of the poet with the "witchery" of Nature, in her summer life, bears us along with him and gives a rare vividness and attraction to his descriptions. PROFESSOR CHAPMAN'S "SONG OF CHARITY" unmistakably discloses true poetic power. We regret that the plan of the poem and of this work, alike preclude our placing any fair specimen of it before our readers.

II.

With noiseless paddle-dip we glide
Along the bay's dark-fringèd side,
Then out, amidst the waters wide!

With us there floated here last night
Wild threatening waves with foam-caps white,
But these have now spent all their might.

We knew they would not injure us,
Those tossing waves, so boisterous—
And where is now their fret and fuss?

Only a ripple wrinkleth now
The summer lake—and plashes low
Against the boat, in fitful flow.

III.

Still callest thou, thou Whip-poor-Will!
When dropped the moon behind the hill
I heard thee, and I hear thee still.

But mingled with thy plaintive cry
A wilder sound comes ebbing by,
Out of the pine-woods, solemnly.

It dies—and then from tree to tree
Deep breathings pass, and seem to be
The murmurs of a mighty sea.

But hark! The owl's cry comes anew—
Piercing the dark pine-forest through,
With its long too-hoo, too-hoo!

IV.

Swifter and swifter, on we go;
For though the breeze but feigns to blow,
Its kisses greet us, soft and low.

But with us now, and side by side,
Striving awhile for place of pride,
A silent, dusky form doth glide.

Though swift and light the birch-canoe,
It cannot take the palm from you,
My little boat, so trim and true.

"Indian! where away to-night?"
"Homewards I wend: yon beacon light
Shines out for me—good night!" "Good night!"

V.

Shorewards again we glide—and go
Where the sumach shadows flow
Across the purple calm below.

There, hidden voices all night long
Keep up, the sedgy creeks among,
The murmurs of their summer song—

A song most soft and musical—
Like the dulled voice of distant fall,
Or winds that through the pine-tops call.

And where the dusky swamp lies dreaming,
Shines the fire-flies' fitful gleaming—
Through the cedars—dancing, streaming!

VI.

Who hides in yonder dusky tree,
Where but the bats awake should be,
And with his whistling mocketh me?

Such quaint, quick pipings—two-and-two:
Half a whistle, half a coo:
Ah, Master Tree-Frog, gare-à-vous!

The owls on noiseless wing gloom by
Beware, lest one a glimpse espy
Of your grey coat and jewelled eye—

And so, good night!—We glide anew
Where shows the lake its softest blue,
With mirrored star-points sparkling through.

VII.

The lights upon the distant shore
That shone so redly, shine no more:
The Indian-fisher's toil is o'er.

And deepening in the eastern skies,
Where up and up new stars arise,
A pearly lustre softly lies.

Thy witchery waneth. Fare-thee-well,
O Summer Night! Thy tender spell
Within my dreams long time will dwell—

And paint, in many a distant scene,
The lake—the shore—the forest green,
"The marks of that which once hath been."

VIGER-SQUARE.

GEORGE MARTIN.

Here in this quiet garden shade,
  Whose blossoms spread their bloom before me,
The world's gay cheats,—Life's masquerade,
Like evil ghosts from memory fade,
  And calm and holy thoughts come o'er me.

Ambrosial haunt; the orient light
  Falls golden on thy soft seclusion;
And like the lone and shadowy night,
Grim care, abashed, has taken flight,
  And joys gleam forth in rich profusion.

These odorous flowers that feast the bee,
  Those mimic fountains sunward leaping,
And yon red rowans on the tree,
That bring my childhood back to me,
  With hallowed scenes of Memory's keeping.

All these, and more, with beauty clad,
  Invite the City's weary mortals—
The pale-faced maid, the widow sad,
And sinking merchant, growing mad,
  To muse within these peaceful portals.

Here is the stone that sages sought,
  Here the famed lamp of blest Alladden;
Objects that tell ambitious thought,
"All that thy greed hath ever caught
  Cannot like us, console and gladden."

THE CHAUDIÈRE FALLS.

EVAN M'COLL.

Where the Ottawa pours its magnificent tide
Through forests primeval, dark-waving and wide,
There's a scene that for grandeur has scarcely a peer,
'Tis the wild, roaring rush of the mighty Chaudière.

On, onward it dashes—an ocean of spray;
How madly it lashes the rocks in its way!
Like the onset of hosts, when spear breaks against spear,
Is th' omnipotent sweep of the mighty Chaudière.

Evermore, loud as thunder the welkin that rends,
Hark that anthem sublime which to Heaven ascends!
Those dark crags in its path seem to quiver with fear;
They may well dread the shock of the mighty Chaudière!

The pround conqueror's might is the boast of a day;
Thine, river majestic! endureth for aye.
Strange thought, that just thus upon Time's infant ear
Came the God-speaking voice of the mighty Chaudière.

Though, for lips uninspired, it seems almost a crime
To be aught else than mute by a scene so sublime;
Could I paint as I *feel* while I gaze on it here,
How immortal in song were the mighty Chaudière!

BRITANNIA.

ALEXANDER M'LACHLAN.

All hail, my country! hail to thee,
Thou birthplace of the brave and free;
Thou ruler upon land and sea:
Britannia!

No thing of change, no mushroom state;
In wisdom thou cans't work and wait;
Or wield the thunderbolts of Fate:
Britannia!

Oh, nobly hast thou play'd thy part;
What struggles of the head and heart
Have gone to make thee what thou art,
Britannia!

What tho' thy manners may be gruff,
Thy native virtues rude and rough;
Yet is thy heart the sterling stuff,
Britannia!

Great mother of the mighty dead!
Sir Walter sang, and Nelson bled,
To weave a garland for thy head,
Britannia!

And Watt, the great magician, wrought,
And Shakespeare ranged the realms of thought,
And Newton soared, and Cromwell fought,
Britannia!

And Milton's high seraphic art,
And Bacon's head and Burns' heart,
Are glories that shall ne'er depart,
Britannia!

These are the soul of thy renown;
The gems immortal in thy crown;
The suns that never shall go down—
Britannia!

Still lie thy path in truth divine,
Held sacred by thy seal and sign;
And power and glory shall be thine,
Britannia!

BROCK.

CHARLES SANGSTER.

(*Oct.* 13*th*, 1859.*)

One voice, one people,—one in heart
And soul, and feeling, and desire!
Re-light the smouldering martial fire,
Sound the mute trumpet, strike the lyre,
The hero deed cannot expire,
The dead still play their part.

Raise high the monumental stone!
A nation's fealty is theirs,
And we are the rejoicing heirs,
The honored sons of sires whose cares
We take upon us unawares,
As freely as our own.

---

* The day of the inauguration of the new Monument on Queenston Heights.

We boast not of the victory,
    But render homage, deep and just,
    To his—to their—immortal dust,
    Who proved so worthy of their trust
    No lofty pile nor sculptured bust
        Can herald their degree.

No tongue need blazon forth their fame—
    The cheers that stir the sacred hill
    Are but mere promptings of the will
    That conquered then, that conquers still;
    And generations yet shall thrill
        At Brock's remembered name.

Some souls are the Hesperides
    Heaven sends to guard the golden age,
    Illuming the historic page
    With records of their pilgrimage;
    True Martyr, Hero, Poet, Sage:
        And he was one of these.

Each in his lofty sphere sublime
    Sits crowned above the common throng,
    Wrestling with some Pythonic wrong,
    In prayer, in thunder, thought, or song;
    Briareus-limbed, they sweep along,
        The Typhons of the time.

IN MEMORIAM OF OCTOBER 25, 1854.

Written on the occasion of the Balaklava Festival.

JOHN READE.

Oh! say not that the chivalry,
  That our brave fathers led
To noble deeds of bravery,
  In us their sons is dead!
For the same blood that leaped of yore,
  Upon the battle plains
Of Crescy and of Agincourt,
  Still leaps within our veins.

The times are changed; the arts of peace
  Are cherished more than then,
But until wars for ever cease,
  Our country shall have men
To draw the sword for country's good,
   To battle for the right,
To shed their heart's best drop of blood
  In many a hard fought fight.

All honour to the good and brave
  Who fought in days of old,
And shame upon the sordid knave
  Whose heart 's so dull and cold,
As not to feel an honest glow
  Of patriotic pride,
When he is told that long ago
  Such heroes lived and died.

But here, to-night, we meet to tell,
Around the festal board,
Of those, who, to oppression quell,
As bravely drew the sword,
Who blenched not at the thought of death,
But at their country's call,
Were willing to resign their breath
Unto the Lord of all.

And some are here with us to-night,
Who, on that glorious day,
For God's and for a nation's right,
Fought in that bloody fray;
Who, fearless, mid the cannon's din,
Charged with that hero-band,
That with their own heart's-blood did win
Fame for their native land.

But some beneath the Eastern sun
Have found a warrior's rest;
The land on which their fame was won,
Has clasped them to her breast.
And many a heart has sorrowed long
For those that never come;
But God, the God of battles, strong,
Will give their souls a home.

Then let us to their memory give,
A grateful, manly thought,
And, if we prize them, let us live
As nobly as they fought;

Each life is but a battle field,
The Wrong against the Right,
Then think, when Right to Wrong would yield,
Of Balaklava's fight.

THE HIGHLAND EMIGRANT'S LAST FAREWELL.*

(*For Music.*)

EVAN M'COLL.

Adieu my native land—adieu
The banks of fair Lochfyne,
Where the first breath of life I drew,
And would my last resign!
Swift sails the bark that wafteth me
This night from thy loved strand:
O must it be my last of thee,
My dear, dear Fatherland!

O Scotland! o'er the Atlantic roar,
Though fated to depart,
Nor time nor space can e'er efface
Thine image from my heart.

---

*This piece has the true lyrical ring. The deep sensibility, condensed thought, and soul-stirring patriotism of this short ode, would alone vindicate Mr. McColl's right to the title of a true bard. The "*Mountain Minstrèl,*" as he is called in his native land, is much more extensively known as a poet in Scotland, than in Canada. He has the peculiar fortune of having won distinction by his lyrics, both in Gaelic and English. A prominent place has been assigned him in MacKenzie's "*Beauties of Gaelic Poetry, and Lives of the Highland Bards.*" And his poetry has been spoken of in terms of warm admiration by several eminent British critics. He was born in Scotland in 1808, but has resided in Kingston or many years past.

Come weal, come woe—till life's last throe,
My Highland Home shall seem
An Eden bright in Fancy's light,
A Heaven in Memory's dream!

Land of the maids of matchless grace,
The bards of matchless song,
Land of the bold heroic race
That never brook'd a wrong!
Long in the front of nations free
May Scotland proudly stand:
Farewell to thee—farewell to thee,
My dear, dear Fatherland!

HOME-SICK STANZAS.

HON. T. D. M'GEE.

Twice had I sailed the Atlantic o'er,
Twice dwelt an exile in the west;
Twice did kind nature's skill restore
The quiet of my troubled breast—
As moss upon a rifted tree,
So time its gentle cloaking did,
But though the wound no eye could see,
Deep in my heart the barb was hid.

I felt a weight where'er I went—
I felt a void within my brain;
My day-hopes and my dreams were blent
With sable threads of mental pain;

My eye delighted not to look
  On forest old or rapids grand;
The stranger's pride I scarce could brook,
  My heart was in my own dear land.

Where'er I turned, some emblem still
  Roused consciousness upon my track;
Some hill was like an Irish hill,
  Some wild bird's whistle called me back;
A sea-bound ship bore off my peace,
  Between its white, cold wings of woe;
Oh, if I had but wings like these,
  Where my peace went, I too would go.

OUR OWN BROAD LAKE.*

THOMAS M'QUEEN.

We cannot boast of high green hills,
Of proud bold cliffs, where eagles gather—
Of moorland glen and mountain rills,
That echo to the red-bell'd heather.

---

* Mr. McQueen was extensively known through Canada West both as a poet and an editor. He died in July, 1861. The following is extracted from a tribute to his memory, written by W. W. Smith, Esq., editor of the *Owen Sound Times*, and published in that paper at the time of his death.

" Mr. McQueen, before his emigration to Canada, was somewhat known in Scotland as a Poet. Three little volumes, published between 1836 and 1850, were so well received, that they have run thro' three editions each. While finding much to commend in his poetry, we cannot help regretting it took so political a turn; and that Nature, the inexhaustible field of the rural poet, was only courted at intervals. Some twelve years ago, Mr. McQueen commenced the publication of the *Signal* newspaper at Goderich. Afterwards, he removed to Hamilton, and

We cannot boast of mouldering towers,
Where ivy clasps the hoary turret—
Of chivalry in ladies' bowers—
Of warlike fame, and knights who won it—
But had we Minstrel's Harp to wake,
We well might boast our own broad lake!

And we have streams that run as clear,
O'er shelvy rocks and pebbles rushing—
And meads as green, and nymphs as dear,
In rosy beauty sweetly blushing—
And we have trees as tall as towers,
And older than the feudal mansion—
And banks besprent with gorgeous flowers,
And glens and woods with fire-flies glancing,—
But prouder, loftier boast we make,
The beauties of our own broad lake.

The lochs and lakes of other lands,
Like gems, may grace a landscape painting;
Or where the lordly castle stands,
May lend a charm, when charms are wanting;
But ours is deep, and broad, and wide,
With steamships through its waves careering;

---

started a Reform journal, the *Canadian*. Not apparently succeeding so well in Hamilton as at Goderich, he recommenced the *Signal* at the latter place. Mr. McQueen was a vigorous writer, and a forcible though not a polished speaker. Some of his Canadian pieces in verse, which are not numerous, are very beautiful. Of these, we remember " Our own broad Lake," and others. He entered heartily, though too late in life to effect much with his own pen, into the plans of those who were and are seeking to established and build up a native literature among us. Some years ago, he ended an editorial on the subject, with the earnest appeal, " Will *nobody* write a few songs for Canada?"—" Owen Sound Times," July, 1861.

And far upon its ample tide,
The barque its devious course is steering;
While hoarse and loud the billows brake
On islands of our own broad lake!

Immense, bright lake! I trace in thee
An emblem of the mighty ocean;
And in thy restless waves I see
Nature's eternal law of motion;
And fancy sees the Huron Chief
Of the dim past, kneel to implore thee—
With Indian awe he seeks relief,
In pouring homage out before thee;
And I, too, feel my reverence wake,
As gazing on our own broad lake!

I cannot feel as I have felt,
When life with hope and fire was teeming;
Nor kneel as I have often knelt
At beauty's shrine, devoutly dreaming.
Some younger hand must strike the string,
To tell of Huron's awful grandeur:
Her smooth and moonlight slumbering,
Her tempest voices loud as thunder;
Some loftier lyre than mine must wake,
To sing our own broad gleaming lake!

CANADA.

PAMELIA S. VINING.

Fair land of peace! to Britain's rule and throne
Adherent still, yet happier than alone,
And free as happy, and as brave as free.
Proud are thy children,—justly proud, of thee:—

Thou hast no streams renowned in classic lore,
No vales where fabled heroes moved of yore,
No hills where Poesy enraptured stood,
No mythic fountains, no enchanted wood;
But unadorned, rough, cold, and often stern,
The *careless eye* to other lands might turn,
And seek, where nature's bloom is more intense,
Softer delights to charm the eye of sense.

But we who know thee, proudly point the hand
Where thy broad rivers roll serenely grand—
Where, in still beauty 'neath our northern sky,
Thy lordly lakes in solemn grandeur lie—
Where old Niagara's awful voice has given
The floods' deep anthem to the ear of heaven—
Through the long ages of the vanished past;
Through Summer's bloom and Winter's angry blast,—
Nature's proud utterance of unwearied song,
Now, as at first, majestic, solemn, strong,
And ne'er to fail, till the archangel's cry
Shall still the million tones of earth and sky,
And send the shout to ocean's farthest shore:—
'Be hushed ye voices!—time shall be no more!'

Few are the years that have sufficed to change
This whole broad land by transformation strange,
Once far and wide the unbroken forests spread
Their lonely wastes, mysterious and dread—
Forests, whose echoes never had been stirred
By the sweet music of an English word,
Where only rang the red-browed hunter's yell,
And the wolf's howl through the dark sunless dell.

Now fruitful fields and waving orchard trees
Spread their rich treasures to the summer breeze.
Yonder, in queenly pride, a city stands,
Whence stately vessels speed to distant lands;
Here smiles a hamlet through embowering green,
And there, the statelier village-spires are seen;
Here by the brook-side clacks the noisy mill,
There, the white homestead nestles to the hill;
The modest school-house here flings wide its door
To smiling crowds that seek its simple lore;
There, Learning's statelier fane of massive walls
Woos the young aspirant to classic halls;
And bids him in her hoarded treasures, find
The gathered wealth of all earth's gifted minds.

Here too, we see, in primal freshness still,
The cool, calm forest nodding on the hill,
And o'er the quiet valley, clustering green,
The tall trees linked in brotherhood serene,
Feeding from year to year the soil below,
Which shall, in time, with golden harvests glow,
And yield more wealth to Labor's sturdy hands
Than fabled Eldorado's yellow sands.

Where once, with thund'ring din, in years bygone,
The heavy waggon labored slowly on,
Through dreary swamps by rudest causeway spanned,
With shaggy cedars dark on either hand—
Where wolves oft howled in nightly chorus drear,
And boding owls mocked the lone traveller's fear—
Now, o'er the stable Rail, the Iron-horse
Sweeps proudly on, in his exultant course,

Bearing, in his impetuous flight along,
The freighted car with all its living throng,
At speed which rivals in its onward flight
The bird's free wing through azure fields of light.

Wealth of the forest—treasures of the hills—
Majestic rivers,—fertilizing rills,—
Expansive lakes, rich vales, and sunny plains,
Vast fields where yet primeval nature reigns,
Exhaustless treasures of the teeming soil—
These loudly call to enterprising Toil.

Nor vainly call. From lands beyond the sea,
Strong men have turned, O Canada! to thee,—
Turned from their fathers' graves, their native shore,
Smiling to scorn the floods' tempestuous roar,
Gladly to find where broader, ampler room
Allured their steps,—a happy Western home.

The toil-worn peasant looked with eager eyes
O'er the blue waters, to those distant skies;
Where no one groaned 'neath unrequited toil;
Where the strong laborer might own the soil
On which he stood; and, in his manhood's strength,
Smile to behold his growing fields at length;—
Where his brave sons might easily obtain
The lore for which their father sighed in vain,
And, in a few short seasons, take their stand
Among the learned and gifted of the land.

Could ocean-barriers avail to keep
That yearning heart in lands beyond the deep?

No !—the sweet vision of a home—his own,
Haunted his days of toil, his midnights lone ;
Till, gath'ring up his little earthly store,
Boldly he sought this far-off Western shore ;
In a few years to realize far more
Than in his wildest dreams he hoped before.

We cannot boast those skies of milder ray,
'Neath which the orange mellows day by day ;
Where the Magnolia spreads her snowy flowers,
And Nature revels in perennial bowers ;—
Here, Winter holds his long and solemn reign,
And madly sweeps the desolated plain ;—
But Health and Vigor hail the wintry strife,
With all the buoyant glow of happy life ;
And by the blazing chimney's cheerful hearth,
Smile at the blast 'mid songs and household mirth ;

Here, Freedom looks o'er all these broad domains,
And hears no heavy clank of servile chains ;
Here man, no matter what his skin may be,
Can stand erect, and proudly say, I'M FREE !'—
No crouching slaves cower in our busy marts,
With straining eyes and anguish-riven hearts.

The beam that gilds alike the palace walls
And lowly hut, with genial radiance falls
On peer and peasant,—but the humblest here
Walks in the sunshine, free as is the peer.
Proudly he stands with muscle strong and free,
The serf—the slave of no man, doomed to be.
His own, the arm the heavy axe that wields ;
His own, the hands that till the summer fields ;

His own, the babes that prattle in the door;
His own, the wife that treads the cottage floor;
All the sweet ties of life to him are sure;
All the proud *rights* of MANHOOD are secure.

Fair land of peace!—O may'st thou ever be
Even as now the land of LIBERTY!
Treading serenely thy bright upward road,
Honored of nations, and approved of God!
On thy fair front emblazoned clear and bright—
FREEDOM, FRATERNITY, AND EQUAL RIGHT!

SONG FOR CANADA.

CHARLES SANGSTER.

Sons of the race whose sires
Aroused the martial flame,
That filled with smiles
The triune Isles,
Through all their heights of fame!
With hearts as brave as theirs,
With hopes as strong and high,
We'll ne'er disgrace
The honored race
Whose deeds can never die.
Let but the rash intruder dare
To touch our darling strand,
The martial fires
That thrilled our sires
Would flame throughout the land.

Our lakes are deep and wide,
Our fields and forests broad;
    With cheerful air
    We'll speed the share,
And break the fruitful sod;
Till blest with rural peace,
Proud of our rustic toil,
    On hill and plain
    True kings we'll reign,
The victors of the soil.
  But let the rash intruder dare
    To touch our darling strand,
      The martial fires
      That thrilled our sires
Would light him from the land.

Health smiles with rosy face
Amid our sunny dales,
    And torrents strong
    Fling hymn and song
Through all the mossy vales;
Our sons are living men,
Our daughters fond and fair;
    A thousand isles
    Where Plenty smiles,
Make glad the brow of Care.
  But let the rash intruder dare
    To touch our darling strand,
      The martial fires
      That thrilled our sires
Would flame throughout the land.

And if in future years
One wretch should turn and fly,
Let weeping Fame
Blot out his name
From Freedom's hallowed sky;
Or should our sons e'er prove
A coward, traitor race,—
Just heaven! frown
In thunder down,
T'avenge the foul disgrace!
But let the rash intruder dare
To touch our darling strand,
The martial fires
That thrilled our sires
Would light him from the land.

THE FOREST.

(From "Song of Charity.")

E. J. CHAPMAN.

The Forest's faery solitude,
The violet's haunt be mine:
Where call the free in merry mood
From dawn till day's deline!
All gentle creatures gather there
From leafy nest and mossy lair:
The little snakelet, golden and green,
The pointed grass glides swift between;
And there the quaint-eyed lizards play
Throughout the long bright summer-day—

Under the leaves in the gold sun-rain,
To and fro, they gleam and pass,
As the soft wind stirs the grass
A moment, and then sleeps again.
And there, the noontides, dream the deer
Close couchèd, where, with crests upcurled,
The fragrant ferns a forest rear
Within the outer forest-world.
And many a petalled star peeps through
The ferny brake, when breathe anew
The soft wind-pantings. And there too,
The hare and the tiny leveret
Betake them, and their fears forget—
Lazily watching with soft brown eye
The laden bees go sailing by,
With many a bright-winged company
Of glittering forms that come and go,
Like twinkling waves in ceaseless flow,
Across those dreamy depths below.
And high above on the bending bough,
Its gush of song unloosens now
Some forest-bird. Wild, clear, and free
Up-swells the joyous melody
In proud, quick bursts: and then, anon,
In the odorous silence, one by one
The thick notes drop, but do not die:
For through the hush, the soul keeps on
With a music of its own—
So runs the forest minstrelsy!
One other sound there soundeth only
Out of the distance dim and lonely:

Out of the pine-depths, murmuring ever,
Floweth the voice of the flowing river:
"Hither"—so seemeth it—"Hither, O ye!
Whose toil is over, whose task is done,
Whose soul the wearisome world would shun—
Come hither to me!"

THE RAPID.

CHARLES SANGSTER.

All peacefully gliding,
The waters dividing,
The indolent bátteau moved slowly along,
The rowers, light-hearted,
From sorrow long parted,
Beguiled the dull moments with laughter and song:
"Hurrah for the Rapid! that merrily, merrily
Gambols and leaps on its tortuous way;
Soon we will enter it, cheerily, cheerily,
Pleased with its freshness, and wet with its spray."

More swiftly careering,
The wild Rapid nearing,
They dash down the stream like a terrified steed;
The surges delight them,
No terrors affright them,
Their voices keep pace with the quickening speed:
"Hurrah for the Rapid! that merrily, merrily
Shivers its arrows against us in play;
Now we have entered it, cheerily, cheerily,
Our spirits as light as its feathery spray."

Fast downward they're dashing,
Each fearless eye flashing,
Though danger awaits them on every side;
Yon rock—see it frowning!
They strike—they are drowning!
But downward they speed with the merciless tide:
No voice cheers the Rapid, that angrily, angrily
Shivers their bark in its maddening play;
Gaily they entered it—heedlessly recklessly,
Mingling their lives with its treacherous spray!

FALL.

ISIDORE G. ASCHER.

I hear the sobbing rain,
As if the Heavens weep at Autumn's breath;
I see the leaves of summer fall again,
Their beauty changed in death.

The idle wind is still,
A spectral vapor haunts the barren earth;
Upon our teeming joys there comes a chill—
The chill of Winter's dearth.

What if the tinted woods
With outward loveliness are gay and fair,
As if around them blushing Summer broods,
Yearning to linger there!

What if their beauteousness
At death's cold touch is strangely glorified!
Their leaves will crumble soon to nothingness,
Or else be swept aside.

Their change is type of all,
  The hectic loveliness forbodes decay,
Steeped with a dying glow before they fall
  To mingle with the clay.

All that we love and prize,
  Changeth like leaves upon our toilsome way;
Man's hoarded wealth, but dust before his eyes,
  Passing, like life, away.

O leaves and blossoms, fall!
  An after-life shall rise from out the gloom;
The Autumn mists are but the outward pall,
  That hides perennial bloom.

O children of decay!
  Swept by the blast and trodden by the rain,
Your scattered dust shall eloquently say,
  That naught will fall in vain.

THE MAPLE.

REV. H. F. DARNELL, M.A.

All hail to the broad-leaved Maple!
  With its fair and changeful dress—
A type of our youthful country
  In its pride and loveliness;
Whether in Spring or Summer,
  Or in the dreary Fall,
'Mid Nature's forest children,
  She's fairest of them all.

Down sunny slopes and valleys
  Her graceful form is seen,
Her wide, umbrageous branches
  The sun-burnt reaper screen;
'Mid the dark-browed firs and cedars
  Her livelier colors shine,
Like the dawn of a brighter future
  On the settler's hut of pine.

She crowns the pleasant hill top,
  Whispers on breezy downs,
And casts refreshing shadows
  O'er the streets of our busy towns;
She gladdens the aching eye-ball,
  Shelters the weary head,
And scatters her crimson glories
  On the graves of the silent dead.

When Winter's frosts are yielding
  To the sun's returning sway,
And merry groups are speeding
  To sugar-woods away,
The sweet and welling juices,
  Which form their welcome spoil,
Tell of the teeming plenty
  Which here waits honest toil.

When sweet-voiced Spring, soft-breathing,
  Breaks Nature's icy sleep,
And the forest boughs are swaying
  Like the green waves of the deep;

In her fair and budding beauty,
  A fitting emblem she
Of this our land of promise,
  Of hope, of liberty.

And when her leaves, all crimson,
  Droop silently and fall,
Like drops of life-blood welling
  From a warrior brave and tall,
They tell how fast and freely
  Would her children's blood be shed,
Ere the soil of our faith and freedom
  Should echo a foeman's tread.

Then hail to the broad-leaved Maple
  With her fair and changeful dress—
A type of our youthful country
  In its pride and loveliness;
Whether in Spring or Summer,
  Or in the dreary Fall,
'Mid Nature's forest children:
  She's fairest of them all.

CANADA'S WELCOME.

HELEN. M. JOHNSON.

A nation's hearty welcome take,
  Heir to a mighty throne;
Thrice welcome! for old England's sake,
  Thy mother's, and thine own.

From crowded street, from hillside green,
  From fair Canadian vales,
The prayer goes up—God bless the Queen!
  God bless the Prince of Wales!

The rich and poor, the great and small
  Their voices join as one;
Victoria's name is dear to all,
  So is Victoria's Son.

Their tribute other queens have laid
  Upon the land and sea;
But never earthly monarch swayed
  So many hearts as she.

And for her young and gallant heir
  A kindred love prevails;
God hear a nation's fervent prayer!
  God bless the Prince of Wales!

INDIAN SUMMER.*

MRS. MOODIE.

By the purple haze that lies
  On the distant rocky height,
By the deep blue of the skies,
  By the smoky amber light,

---

*Mrs. Moodie is too extensively known to the Canadian public, to require any notice from our pen. Although much better known as a writer of prose, than as a poet, yet many of her poems display great naturalness and purity of style, and a genuine love of Nature in her varied phases, which qualifies her to describe natural scenery with graphic truthfulness. This vivid description of Indian Summer will call up to the mind of every Canadian reader, those tranquil autumn days, "when Nature on her throne sits dreaming."

Through the forest arches streaming
Where Nature on her throne sits dreaming,
And the sun is scarcely gleaming,
  Through the cloudlets, snowy white,—
Winter's lovely herald greets us,
Ere the ice-crowned tyrant meets us—

A mellow softness fills the air,—
  No breeze on wanton wing steals by,
To break the holy quiet there,
  Or makes the waters fret and sigh,
Or the golden alders shiver,
That bend to kiss the placid river,
Flowing on, and on forever,
  But the little waves are sleeping,
  O'er the pebbles slowly creeping,
  That last night were flashing, leaping,
Driven by the restless breeze,
In lines of foam beneath yon trees—

Dressed in robes of gorgeous hue,
  Brown and gold with crimson blent;
The forest to the waters blue
  Its own enchanting tints has lent;—
In their dark depths, life-like glowing,
We see a second forest growing,
Each pictured leaf and branch bestowing
A fairy grace to that twin wood,
Mirror'd within the crystal flood.

'Tis pleasant now in forest shades;—
  The Indian hunter strings his bow,

To track through dark entangling glades
The antler'd deer and bounding doe,—
  Or launch at night the birch canoe,
To spear the finny tribes that dwell
On sandy bank in weedy cell,
Or pool the fisher knows right well—
Seen by the red and vivid glow
Of pine-torch at his vessel's bow.

This dreamy Indian-summer day,
  Attunes the soul to tender sadness;
We love—but joy not in the ray—
  It is not Summer's fervid gladness,
But a melancholy glory
  Hovering softly round decay,
Like swan that sings her own sad story,
  Ere she floats in death away.

The day declines, what splendid dyes,
  In fleckered waves of crimson driven,
Float o'er the saffron sea that lies
  Glowing within the western heaven!
  O it is a peerless even!
See the broad red sun has set,
But his rays are quivering yet
Through Nature's veil of violet,—
  Streaming bright o'er lake and hill;
  But earth and forest lie so still,
  It sendeth to the heart a chill,
We start to check the rising tear,
'Tis beauty sleeping on her bier—

THE LAKE OF THE THOUSAND ISLES.

(*For Music.*)

EVAN M'COLL.

Though Missouri's tide majestic may glide,
  There's a curse on the soil it laves;
The Ohio too, may be fair, but who
  Would sojourn in a land of slaves?
Be my prouder lot a Canadian cot,
  And the bread of a freeman's toil;
Then hurrah for the Land of the forests grand,
  And the Lake of the Thousand Isles!

I would seek no wealth at the cost of health,
  'Mid the city's din and strife;
More I love the grace of fair Nature's face,
  And the calm of a woodland life:
I would shun the road by Ambition trod,
  And the lore which the heart defiles;—
Then hurrah for the Land of the forests grand,
  And the Lake of the Thousand Isles!

O away, away, I would gladly stray
  Where the freedom I love is found;
Where the Pine and Oak by the woodman's stroke
  Are disturb'd in their ancient bound:
Where the gladsome swain reaps the golden grain,
  And the trout from the stream beguiles;
Then hurrah for the Land of the forests grand,
  And the Lake of the Thousand Isles!

THE THOUSAND ISLANDS.

CHARLES SANGSTER.

Here the Spirit of beauty keepeth
  Jubilee for evermore;
Here the voice of gladness leapeth,
  Echoing from shore to shore.
O'er the hidden watery valley,
  O'er each buried wood and glade,
Dances our delighted galley,
  Through the sunlight and the shade—
Dances o'er the granite cells,
Where the soul of beauty dwells:

Here the flowers are ever springing,
  While the summer breezes blow;
Here the Hours are ever clinging,
  Loitering before they go;
Playing around each beauteous islet,
  Loath to leave the sunny shore,
Where, upon her couch of violet,
  Beauty sits for evermore—
Sits and smiles by day and night,
Hand in hand with pure Delight.

Here the Spirit of beauty dwelleth
  In each palpitating tree,
In each amber wave that welleth
  From its home beneath the sea;
In the moss upon the granite,
  In each calm, secluded bay,

With the zephyr trains that fan it
  With their sweet breaths all the day—
On the waters, on the shore,
Beauty dwelleth evermore!

APPROACH TO QUEBEC.

W. KIRBY.

At length they spy huge Tourment, sullen-browed,
Bathe his bald forehead in a passing cloud;
The Titan of the lofty Capes that gleam
In long succession down the mighty stream.
When lo! Orleans emerges to the sight,
And woods and meadows float in liquid light:
Rude Nature doffs her savage mountain dress,
And all her sternness melts to loveliness.
On either hand stretch fields of richest green,
With glittering village spires and groves between;
And snow-white cots adorn the fertile plain,
Where grazing flocks or distant moving wain,
Or human figure, though but half descried,
Pour life upon the landscape far and wide.

Now passed the Island portal; opens free
A glorious bay, fair as a summer sea;
Where boats and birds expand their mingled wings,
And many a princely ship at anchor swings,
While the reclining shore's immense concave
Of fields and gardens, drinks the crystal wave,
And sweeps away, till round th' horizon seen,
Enfolding hills, the beauteous vision screen.

Afar, Quebec exalts her crest on high,
Her rocks and battlements invade the sky;
The pride of Canada, her strength and head;
England's assurance and Columbia's dread.
Her rampired rock appears 'mid nature's charms,
Like Mars reposing in fair Venus' arms,
His ponderous spear with flowery garlands hung,
Peace in his eye and friendship on his tongue.

Softly the king of day reclining, spreads
His mantle o'er the crispèd stream, and sheds
His slantant rays, rich as the golden shower
That ushered Jove into the Argive bower.
'Neath rows of trees the whitened houses stand,
The fisher's boats lie basking on the strand;
The light caleche speeds o'er the dusty road,
And peasants trudge beneath their market load.

O, glorious sight! as golden sunset showers
Athwart the long-drawn walls and lofty towers;
Corruscant rays play round the cross topped spires
And gild each salient point with shimmering fires.
Half screened 'mid countless masts, an endless maze
Of quays and roofs spring from the watery haze;
While on the Bay's broad bosom, far and wide,
The anchored fleets of commerce proudly ride.
Huge cliffs above, precipitous that frown,
Like Atlas bend beneath another town,
Where all along the grey embrasured steep
In grim repose the watchful cannon peep,
Tall spires, and domes, and turrets shine afar
Behind the archèd gates, and mounds of war,

While proud Cape Diamond towers above them all,
With aerial glacis and embattled wall;
Till on the loftiest point where birds scarce rise,
Old England's standard floats amid the skies.

O! glorious spot! The Briton's boast and pride,
Where armies battled and where heroes died,
Where gallant Wolfe led his devoted band,
Rejoiced in death, and waved his dying hand;
'Mid cheers of Victory rung from side to side,
The hero smiled content, and calmly died,
Though few his years and young his lofty fame,
With greenest garlands, England crowns his name,
And on her roll of glory, proudly reads
The eternal records of his mighty deeds.
And noble Montcalm! well thy honoured bier
May claim the tribute of a British tear.
Although the lilies from these ramparts fell,
Thy name, immortal with great Wolfe's shall dwell:
Like him, the consciousness of duty done,
Soothed thy last pang, and cheered thy setting sun.

THE PLAINS OF ABRAHAM.

CHARLES SANGSTER.

I stood upon the Plain,
That had trembled when the slain
Hurled their proud, defiant curses at the battle-heated foe,
When the steed dashed right and left,
Through the bloody gaps he cleft,
When the bridle-rein was broken, and the rider was laid low.

What busy feet had trod
Upon the very sod
Where I marshalled the battalions of my fancy to my aid!
And I saw the combat dire,
Heard the quick, incessant fire,
And the cannons' echoes startling the reverberating glade.

I heard the chorus dire,
That jarred along the lyre
On which the hymn of battle rung, like surgings of the wave.
When the storm, at blackest night,
Wakes the ocean in affright,
As it shouts its mighty pibroch o'er some shipwrecked vessel's grave.

I saw the broad claymore
Flash from its scabbard, o'er
The ranks that quailed and shuddered at the close and fierce attack;
When Victory gave the word,
Auld Scotia drew the sword,
And with arm that never faltered drove the brave defenders back.

I saw two great chiefs die,
Their last breaths like the sigh
Of the zephyr-sprite that wantons on the rosy lips of morn;
No envy-poisoned darts,
No rancour, in their hearts,
To unfit them for their triumph over death's impending scorn.

And as I thought and gazed,
My soul, exultant, praised

The Power to whom each mighty act and victory are due,
For the saint-like Peace that smiled
Like a heaven-gifted child,
And for the air of quietude that steeped the distant view.

Oh, rare, divinest life
Of peace, compared with Strife!
Yours is the truest splendor, and the most enduring fame;
All the glory ever reaped
Where the fiends of battle leaped,
Is harsh discord to the music of your undertoned acclaim.

ALMA.

ANNIE L. WALKER.

There comes a murmur o'er the sea of mingled joy and woe,
From where, O Alma! stained with blood, thy rapid waters flow;
The shout of triumph blends with sobs of anguish, stern and deep,
Yet love and pride have mighty power to comfort those who weep.

And we, who, wand'ring far from home, in distant lands abide,
Forget not those who on thy banks have nobly fought and died;
The hope and flower of each fair land together, foes no more,
Brothers in death lie side by side, upon thy fated shore.

The laurels, planted in our hearts and watered by our tears,
Shall live to mark their honoured graves through many passing years;
And though the land in darkness lie their resting place around,
Yet, where they sleep—the brave and free—is consecrated ground.

Rejoice, O England! 'mid thy tears, rejoice to hear it told
How well thy sons maintained the fame their fathers won of old;
To show the world that Peace may shed her blessings o'er the land,
Nor weaken one courageous heart, nor rear one feeble hand.

And thou, fair France! e'en by the bier where sleeps thy gallant chief,
Let joy and exultation find a place amid thy grief;
Nobly he fills a soldier's grave, although not in the strife,
But worn by sickness long endured, he yielded up his life.

Oh, may the memory of the hearts grown cold by Alma's shore,
Draw closer yet the bands of love between us evermore;
England and France, together joined, resistless in the fight,
May conquer still for those oppressed, may still defend the right.

THE TWOFOLD VICTORY.

CHARLES SANGSTER.

By the famous Alma River
  Knelt a Warrior, brave and young,
Through his veins ran Death's cold shiver,
  On his lips his last breath hung;
Far above him rolled the battle,
  Downward rolled to Alma's wave,
Downward, through the crash and rattle,
  Came the cheering of the brave.

"Comrades," said he, rising slowly,
  Kneeling on one bended knee,
"Comrades," said he, feebly, lowly,
  "Is that cheer for Victory?"

"Yes!—they fly!—the foe is flying!"
  "Comrades," said he, ardently,
"Cheer for me, for I am dying,
  Cheer them on to Victory!"

By that blood-encrimsoned River
  Cheered they with a martial pride,
Death's last shaft had left its quiver,
  And the Warrior, smiling, died.
Faintly his last cheer was given,
  Feebly his last breath went free,
And his spirit passed to Heaven
  On the wings of Victory!

THE SOLDIER OF AUVERGNE.

MISS H. A. WILKINS.

'Twas midnight, and the soldier took
  His lone and quiet march;
The moon's bright rays fell gloriously
  Upon the forest arch;
And through that forest's dreary gloom,
  Full twenty leagues away,
The army of the enemy
  Waited the dawn of day.

The watcher listened, for he heard
  The wild-wolf's dismal howl,
A crashing of the underbrush
  Betrayed his wary prowl;

Yet where the branches thickest weave,
  The soldier took his way;
He started—for a band of foes
  Had seized him as their prey.

He was a captive—one strong hand
  Upon his lips did lie,
While in hoarse whispers rung their words,
  "Betray us and you die."
Warm love was nestling at his heart,
  Warm life was in his veins,
One dream of love, of life, of home,
  One dream of captive chains.

'Twas but a moment, and he thought
  Of those who slept around,
Safe and secure while he kept watch
  Upon the sentry ground.
'Twas but a moment, and a flush
  Passed o'er his cheek and brow;
His voice rang on the midnight air,
  "Auvergne! Auvergne! the foe!"

The swords that in the moonlight shone
  Upon his bosom rushed;
And from the dauntless soldier's heart
  Life's streamlets quickly gushed.
Yet ere his beaming eye was closed,
  He saw his brethren's lance;
Trampling down bush and brake, he heard
  The cavalry of France.

He felt strong arms around him placed,
He saw their princely train;
A nation's thanks were in his ears,—
He had not died in vain.
They laid him, while the host pursued
The fast retreating foe,
Beneath that glorious flag for which
He laid himself so low.

O! may it be that when, if e'er,
So dire a fate we claim,
And through our country loud resounds
War's fearful, shuddering name—
Then may our hearts and households yield
Then may our foemen learn,
We have such hearts as sleep beneath
The banner of Auvergne.

THUNDER-STORM IN AUGUST.*

W. KIRBY.

But when fierce August suns careering high
Gaze hot and silent from the brazen sky;
When bird and beast forsake the open glade
And pant all mute within the sultry shade;
When not a breath doth stir the lightest leaf;
And springs and brooks dried up deny relief;

---

*"*The U. E., a Tale of Upper Canada*," published at Niagara in 1859, though not free from occasional bad rhyme, and inharmonious lines, contains some striking descriptions of Canadian scenery, seasons, and life, and many passages of much spirit and force.

While Nature lies exhausted in the throes
Of parching thirst the sharpest of her woes;
Then lo! a small dark cloud all fringed with red,
Above th' horizon lifts its liquid head;
Surveys the scene, and larger grows to view,
While all the legions of the storm pursue.
The muttering thunder with unceasing din
Proclaims the strife of elements within;
And lurid flashes flood the murky clouds,
As faster on they follow, crowds on crowds.

Eclipsed the sun, his fires at once allayed,
Falls o'er the quaking earth, a dreadful shade;
A thousand birds aloft in terror rise,
And seek the safest haunts, with piercing cries:
The leaves, they tremble in the breathless woods
And sighing trees confess th' approaching floods.
At once 'mid clouds of dust and flying leaves
The whirlwind sweeps aloft the scattered sheaves;
Sharp lightning rends the black and marble skies
And thousand-voiced the pealing thunder flies.
The shattered boughs upon the tempest ride;
And rocking forests groan from side to side;
While cataracts of rain in deluge pour,
And sweep the smoking land with ceaseless roar.

The wild tornado passes, and the sun
With golden rays peeps through the clouds of dun,
Green Nature glistens, and the piping bird
Within the dripping grove is fluttering heard;
While down the steaming gullies furrowed wide
The rushing waters pour on every side,

And earth refreshed, emerges from the storm
With smiling face and renovated form.
So oft in human life, when Fortune's blaze
Makes men forgetful of their Maker's praise;
Observe kind Providence with holy ire
Send on that man its purifying fire,
Reverses, poverty, disease and death,
To stay corruption's foul contagious breath,
To keep alive the spark of truth within,
Purge off the brute and cleanse the pitchy sin.

FROST ON THE WINDOW.

MRS. R. A. FAULKNER.

There's not a thing that Nature's hand hath made,
However simple be its outward seeming,
To careless eye or listless ear displayed,
But hath a hidden meaning.

Alike, unto the Saint's or Atheist's ear
The anthem of the woodland choir is given;
One hears "the lark," what doth the other hear?
A hymn of praise to heaven.

The glowing rainbow steals its silent march
Athwart the sky when rain-drops gem the sod,
One sees three gorgeous hues in Heaven's arch,
And one—the law of God.

The winter moon was shining coldly bright:
The birds and leaves had left the trees together,
Save here and there, one, that on some lone height
        Still braved the bitter weather.

And o'er the window crept the hoary frost,
With many a wayward freak and curious antic,
In varied lines, that quaintly blent and crossed
        In tracery romantic.

Here, bloomed a wreath of pure pale flowers,
As hueless as the faded cheek of death;
There, rose tall pinnacles and Gothic towers,
        That melted with a breath.

And trees and foliage rich—the dinted oak,
The willow, wan and still, like settled grief,
The hazel, easy bent, but hardly broke,
        And varying maple leaf—

—That changes still its green or crimson hue
With every season, autumn, spring or summer,
A sycophant which wears a livery new,
        To welcome each new comer.

The gentle moonbeam kissed the silvery pane
With a most sister-like and chaste caress,
As if it fain a fellowship would claim,
        With such pure loveliness.

And still more beautiful, the magic ray
Made all it rested on, leaf, flower and tree,
And lingered there, like innocence at play
        With stainless purity.

Oh beautiful it was to watch them there,
Those varied forms, so gracefully fantastic,
The handiwork, so delicately fair,
Of Nature's fingers plastic.

And as I gazed, methought such sights were given
Not to our gross material senses solely,
But to the soul, like messengers from Heaven,
Prompting pure thoughts and holy.

There's not a thing that Nature's hand hath made,
However simple be its outward seeming,
To careless eye or listless ear displayed,
But hath a hidden meaning.

SNOW.

JENNIE E. HAIGHT.

Snow—snow—fast-falling snow!
Snow on the house-tops—snow in the street—
Snow overhead, and snow under feet—
Snow in the country—snow in the town,
Silently, silently sinking down;
Everywhere, everywhere fast-falling snow,
Dazzling the eyes with its crystalline glow!

Snow—snow—beautiful snow!
How the bells ring o'er the fresh-fallen snow!—
How the bells ring, as the sleighs come and go!

Happy-heart voices peal out on the air,
Joy takes the reins from the dull hand of care;
Singing and laughter, and innocent mirth,
Seem from this beautiful snow to have birth.

Pure, pure, glittering snow!
Oh! to look at it and think of the woe
Hidden to-night 'neath this mantle of snow!
Oh! but to think of the tears that are shed
Over the snow-covered graves of the dead!
Aye, and the anguish more hopeless and keen,
That yearneth in silence o'er *what might have been!*

Snow—snow—chilling, white snow!
Who, as he glides through the bustling street,
Would care to follow the hurrying feet,
Crushing beneath them the chilling white snow—
Bearing up fiercely their burden of woe,
Till, weary and hopeless, they enter in,
Where food and fire are the wages of sin?

Snow—snow—wide-spreading snow!
No haunt is so cheerless, but there it can fall,
Like the mantle of charity, covering all:
Want, with its suffering,—sin, with its shame,
In its purity breathing the thrice blessed name
Of One who, on earth, in sorrow could say—
"The sinning and poor are with you alway."

Oh, brothers, who stand secure in the right,—
Oh, sisters, with fingers so dainty-white,—
Think, as you look on the fast-falling snow—

Think, as you look at the beautiful snow,
Pure, pure, glittering snow—chilling white snow—
Think of the want, and the sin, and the woe,
Crouching to-night 'neath the wide-spreading snow!

Give of your plenty to God's suff'ring poor,
Turn not the lost one away from your door:
For his poor He prepareth blest mansions on high;
Rich in faith, they inherit bright crowns in the sky.
The lost ones, though sunken never so low,
Christ's blood can make them all whiter than snow,
Pure, pure, glittering snow, beautiful snow.

SUNSET SCENE.

PAMELIA S. VINING.

The glorious sun behind the western hills
  Slowly in gorgeous majesty retires,
Flooding the founts and forests, fields and rills,
  With the reflection of his golden fires.
How beauteous all, how calm, how still,
Yon star that trembles on the hill!
Yon crescent moon that raises high
Her beaming horns upon the sky,
  Seem bending down a loving glance
    From the unclouded skies,
  On the green earth that far away
    In solemn beauty lies;
And, like sweet Friendship in affliction's hour,
Grow brighter still the more the shadows lower.

AUTUMN.

JAMES M'CARROLL.

The ripe fields are scattered in eddies of gold
On the verge of the forest that's kindling apace;
And the orchards that dapple the wide-spreading wold,
Through their loopholes of leaves—as we pause to behold—
Flash their beautiful, festival lamps in our face.

And the amber, coned pear, with the peaches flushed ball,
And the sunny-cheeked apple that's crimsoned all o'er,
Blends with pleiads of grapes, that in purple showers fall
Over many a green-muffled trellis and wall,
With a thousand bright fancies and dreams at their core.

And its coralline clusters the mountain ash shakes,
Till they rattle in fiery hail to the ground;
While the briar's red candles are lit in the brakes,
Where the robin besprinkled with glory awakes,
Thrilling out his sweet soul to the echoes around.

And the honey-veined maple, beginning to flout
In the chill morning breadth of the sudden-winged blast,
Soon its deep scarlet leaves shakes so ruthlessly out,
That like clouds of dead butterflies floating about,
They proclaim to the landscape, that summer is past.

IN THE WOODS.

REV. JOHN MAY, M.A.

O! it is sweet, on summer morn,
When flowers the grassy mead adorn,
To wander in the wild wood glen,
The thicket shade, the quivering fen;

To climb the heights and see the spray
Dash'd on the face of toying day;
To hear the distant waters roar,
Or gather pebbles on the shore;
To start the hare, or, with your cur,
To know the partridge by its whirr;
To hear on some tall bough the dove
Utter the soft complaint of love;
Whilst mocking squirrel on lofty limb
Defies you to get up to him;
The chipmonk, too, in nimble style,
Darts tim'rously to the stony pile,—
Sits temptingly a moment there,
Then vanishes into his lair;
Or if, perchance, his house should be
Beneath the root of some tall tree,
He quick descends with sudden squeak;
For him your dog begins to seek:
First snuffs awhile, then tears away
The leaves, the rubbish, and the clay,
With many a howl and rapid scratch,
Intent the little scamp to catch:
Perhaps, while thus engaged, his prey
Makes his escape some other way.
Leaving his foe to dig with pain—
As better folks have done—in vain;
But should the perservering brute
Find him at last beneath the root
The hapless little creature's fate
Is far too mournful to relate!

THE FALLS OF NIAGARA.

E. H. DEWART.

Ere yet I saw the wild magnificence,
Which Nature here with peerless pomp unveils,
A solemn sound—a stern and sullen roar—
By which the earth was tremulously thrilled,
Awoke a flush of deep expectant joy,
Quickening the pulses of my throbbing heart,
And tingling thro' my veins like fire. But here,
Standing upon this rocky ledge, above
The vast abyss which yawns beneath, gazing
In silent awe and rapture, face to face
With this bright vision of unearthly glory,
Which dwarfs all human pageantry and power,
To me this spot is Nature's holiest temple.
The sordid cares, the jarring strifes, and vain
Delights of earth are stilled. The hopes and joys
Which gladden selfish hearts are nothing here.

The massy rocks that sternly tower aloft,
And stem the fury of the wrathful tide—
Th' impetuous leap of the resistless flood,
An avalanche of foaming curbless wrath—
The silent hills, God's tireless sentinels—
The wild and wondrous beauty of thy face,
Which foam and spray enshroud from sight, as if,
Like thy Creator, God, thy glorious face
No mortal eye may see unveiled and live—
Oh! what are noblest works of mortal art,
Column, or arch, or vast cathedral dome,
To these majestic foot-prints of our God!

Unique and peerless in thy radiant might,
Earth has no emblems to portray thy splendor;
Not e'en the bard of Paradise could sing,
All that thy grandeur whispers to the heart
That feels thy power. No words of mortal lips
Can fitly speak the wonder, reverence, joy,—
The wild imaginings, intense and yet serene,
Which now, like spirits from some higher sphere
For whom no earthly tongue has name or type,
Sweep through my soul in waves of surging thought.
My reason struggles with a vague desire
To plunge into thy boiling waves, and blend
My being with thy wild sublimity.
As thy majestic beauty sublimates
My soul, I am ennobled while I gaze,
Warm tears of pensive joy gush from my eyes,
And grateful praise and worship silent swell
Unbidden from my thrilled and ravished breast:
Henceforth this dream of beauty shall be mine—
Daguerreotyped forever on my heart.

Stupendous power! thy thunder's solemn hymn,
Whose voice rebukes the shallow unbeliefs
Of men, is still immutably the same.
Ages ere mortal eyes beheld thy glory,
Thy floods made music for the listening stars,
And angels paused in wonder as they passed:
Thousands, who here have once enraptured stood,
Forgotten lie in death's lone dreamless sleep;
And when each beating heart on earth is stilled,
Thy tide shall roll, unchanged by flight of years,
Bright with the beauty of eternal youth.

Thy face, half-veiled in rainbows, mist and foam,
Awakens thoughts of all the beautiful
And grand of earth, which stand through time and change
As witnesses of God's omnipotence.
The hoary mountain, stern in regal pride,
The birth place of the avalanche of death—
The grand old forests, through whose solemn aisles
The winter winds their mournful requiems chant—
The mighty rivers rolling to the sea—
The thunder's peal—the lightning's awful glare—
The deep, wide sea, whose melancholy dirge,
From age to age yields harmony divine—
The star-lit heavens, magnificent and vast,
Where suns and worlds in fadeless splendor blaze—
ALL terrible and beauteous things create
Are linked in holy brotherhood with thee,
And speak in tones above the din of earth,
Of Him unseen, whose word created all.

God of Niagara! Fountain of life!
At whose omnific word the universe
Arose; whose love upholds all worlds, and guides
Each orb in its mysterious path through space;
Around whose throne the Morning-Stars of light
Bend low in wondering adoration, or
With lofty hymns of love and joy proclaim
Thy power and grace, boundless—immutable!
I, a poor erring worm of earth, a child
Of sin, am all unworthy to behold
This faint reflection of thy glorious power;
How then can I approach thy holy throne?
Or dare to breathe in thine offended ear,

The wants and woes of my polluted heart?
Father of mercy, hear my trembling prayer!
To me let love and light divine be given,
To guide my erring feet in paths of truth,
And purify my dark and sin-stained heart;
That while I muse upon thy glorious works,
And mark the tokens of thy presence here,
I may behold Thyself, and find in Thee
My Strength, my Light, my everlasting Friend.

SUNSET.

J. F. M'DONNELL.

'Tis joy to gaze upon the west,
Where sinks the glorious sun to rest,
Upon the sleeping ocean's breast—
In purple even.
When crimson clouds are backward rolled,
Like some gay banner's broidered fold,
From the wide arch of shaded gold—
As bright as heaven.

The splendor of the evening rays
Upon the rippling water plays,
Far brighter than the jewel's blaze—
Or rich gem's glory.
The Island summit crowned with pines,
Bathed in its gay tints far outshines
The lustre of all fabled shrines—
In song or story.

And gently still the twilight fades,
Beneath the twisted old oak's shades,
And the dim forest's leafy glades—
Are sunk in shadow.
But lingering last the faint grey light
Withdraws its ray—once dazzling bright—
From mountain's crest and rocky height—
From hill and meadow.

Thus when we glide unto our rest—
O may it be when in the west—
The sunset gilds the ocean's breast—
In purple even.
When crimson clouds are backward rolled
From the wide arch of shaded gold,
On some such eve may we behold—
One glimpse of heaven!

MAY.*

ALEXANDER M'LACHLAN,

O sing and rejoice!
Give to gladness a voice;
Shout, a welcome to beautiful May!
Rejoice with the flowers,
And the birds 'mong the bowers,
And away to the green woods, away.

---

* There is in this poem a dancing, sparkling gladness, strikingly in keeping with the exuberant joyousness of the season and scenery it describes. In the introduction to this work, we have expressed our high estimate of Mr. McLachlan's genius. It is no empty laudation to call him the "Burns of Canada." In racy humour, in

O, blithe as the fawn,
Let us dance in the dawn
Of this life-giving glorious day.
'Tis bright as the first
Over Eden that burst;
O welcome, young joy-giving May.

The cataract's horn
Has awakened the morn,
Her tresses are dripping with dew;
O hush thee and hark!
'Tis her herald the lark
That is singing afar in the blue;
Its happy heart's rushing,
In strains mildly gushing,
That reach to the revelling earth,
And sink through the depths
Of the soul, till it leaps
Into raptures far deeper than mirth.

---

natural pathos, in graphic portraiture of character, he will compare favorably with the great peasant bard; while, in moral grandeur and beauty, he frequently strikes higher notes than ever echoed from the harp of Burns. Those who will be most forward to question the propriety of any comparison between Burns and McLachlan, will be just those whom strong national and educational prejudice disqualify for exercising an impartial judgment. Mr. McL. has published, at intervals, three small volumes of poems. The last of these, "*The Emigrant and other poems*," especially, exhibits poetic power of a high order. But in spite of qualities that justly entitled it to a warm reception, and an extensive sale, we learn with regret, that it was so shamefully neglected, that its publication involved the author in financial embarrassment, from which he is not yet fully free. But pioneers, in all departments of activity, must expect to suffer. Mr. McLachlan was born in Scotland, in 1820; and resides at present at Erin, near Guelph. Last year he was appointed by the government to lecture in Great Britain on the advantages of emigrating to this country. He acquitted himself in this mission with great efficiency, for he has the gifts of an orator as well as those of a poet.

All Nature's in keeping,
The live streams are leaping,
And laughing in gladness along;
The great hills are heaving;
The dark clouds are leaving;
The valleys have burst into song.
We'll range through the dells
Of the bonnie blue-bells,
And sing with the streams on their way;
We'll lie in the shades
Of the flower-covered glades,
And hear what the primroses say.

O crown me with flowers,
'Neath the green spreading bowers,
With the gems and the jewels May brings;
In the light of her eyes,
And the depth of her dyes,
We'll smile at the purple of kings!
We'll throw off our years,
With their sorrows and tears,
And time will not number the hours
We'll spend in the woods,
Where no sorrow intrudes,
With the streams and the birds, and the flowers.

NOVEMBER—A DIRGE.

J. R. RAMSAY.

The old oak tree is dying,
The storm-tanned branch of centuries is bare,
The bark is riven from the trunk, and lying,

Distant and near;
The last fair robe of summer leaves is flying,
Withered and sear.

Departing wild birds gather
On the high branches, ere they haste away,
Singing their farewell to the frigid ether,
And fading day,
To sport no more on withered mead or heather;
No longer gay.

And sullenly assuming
His throne, to vindicate the summer past,
Stern Autumn stops the thunder's distant booming,
And lightning's blast;
While from the north the dreary clouds are coming,
Sombre and vast.

The little cricket's singing,
Sounds lonely in the crisp and yellow leaves,
Like by-gone tones of tenderness up-bringing
A thought that grieves:
A bell upon a ruined turret ringing
On Sabbath eves.

The "tempest-loving raven,"
Pilot of storms across the silent sky,
Soars loftily along the heaving heaven,
With doleful cry,
Ut'ring lone dirges. Thistle-beards are driven
Where the winds sigh.

And yet here is a flower
Still lingering, by the changing season spared,
And a lone bird within a leafless bower—
Two friends, who dared
To share the shadows of misfortune's hour,
Though unprepared.

THE FISHERMAN'S LIGHT.

A SONG OF THE BACKWOODS.

MRS. MOODIE.

The air is still—the night is dark—
No ripple breaks the dusky tide,
From isle to isle the fisher's bark,
Like fairy meteor, seems to glide—
Now lost in shade—now flashing bright,
On sleeping wave and forest tree,
We hail with joy the ruddy light,
Which far into the darksome night
Shines red and cheerily.

With spear high poised and steady hand,
The centre of that fiery ray,
Behold the skilful fisher stand,
Prepared to strike the finny prey—
"Now, now!" the shaft has sped below—
Transfixed the shining prize we see,
On swiftly glides the birch canoe—
The woods send back the long halloo
In echoes loud and cheerily!

Around yon bluff whose pine crest hides
The noisy rapids from our sight,
Another bark—another glides—
Red spirits of the murky night—
The bosom of the silent stream
With mimic stars is dotted free,
The tall woods lighten in the beam,
Through darkness shining cheerily.

TO AN OWL.

JOHN MASSIE.

Hoot awa hoolet, alane on the tree,
Hoot awa, bird! are you hooting at me?
Or is it a change in the weather you bring?
Or do you rejoice in the birth o' the Spring?
Or wailing the past sadly mourn o'er thy lot,
Till the depths of the forest re-echo thy note?
When the music of birds and the humming of bees
Are hushed on the breast of the evening breeze;
When Nature is laid in the lap of Repose,
And Harmony reigns in the bosoms of foes;
When the world is asleep, and the last ray of light
Is swept from the earth with the besom of night,—
You are seen on the wing—though we cannot well see,
For thy daylight is darkness, mine darkness to thee;
You are seen on the wing, by the pale moonlight
To flit like a ghost on the shadow of night,
Or perched on a tree are heard nightly to croon,
Thy sorrowful tale to the wandering morn.

O child of the night! cease to echo along
The mournful "too-whoo" of thy midnight song,
Or the sprites of the night will assemble to hear,
Or the elfs o' the wood will be caught in a tear.
Do you mourn in sad numbers a lover's disdain,
Or pour out thy passion in amorous strain?
Oh surely thy notes are the language of care,
Commingled with tenderness, love and despair.
Mayhap the sole friend of thy bosom has fled,
And left thee to wail o'er the bones of the dead;
Or the feathering brood, that so often were pressed
With a motherly tenderness close to thy breast,
Have fled thee ungrateful, and left thee to mourn
O'er thy woes and thy sorrows alone and forlorn.

Hoot awa, hoolet, thy song on the tree
Is wae to my saul, and is tears to my e'e,
For my lot may be dark, and like thee I may mourn
Over joys that have fled and can never return;
Forsaken by friends, and forgotten by foes,
I may sink in the arms of unconscious repose,
May read the last lesson of life's rugged page
With no one to soothe in the sorrows of age.
O child of the night! on thy sentinel tree,
Why not take a lesson of patience from thee?
Why weep o'er the transient woes of a day?
For though dark be my youth, yet my end may be calm,
And the evening of light bathe my sorrows in balm,
And the spirit, long pent in this casket of clay,
Spread its pinions aloft, and go smiling away.

WHIP-POOR-WILL.

ALEXANDER M'LACHLAN.

There is a lonely spirit
  Which wanders thro' the wood,
And tells its mournful story
  In every solitude;
It comes abroad at eventide
  And hangs beside the rill,
And murmurs to the ear of night
  "Whip-poor-will."

Oh 'tis a hapless spirit
  In likeness of a bird,
A grief that cannot utter
  Another woeful word,
A soul that seeks for sympathy,
  A woe that won't be still,
A wandering sorrow murmuring
  "Whip-poor-will."

HAUNTS OF A DEMON.

(*From Saul.*)

CHARLES HEAVYSEGE.

The Jewish king now walks at large and sound,
Yet of our emissary Malzah hear we nothing:
Go now, sweet spirit, and, if need be, seek
This world all over for him:—find him out,
Be he within the bounds of earth and hell.

He is a most erratic spirit, so
May give thee trouble (as I give thee time)
To find him, for he may be now diminished,
And at the bottom of some silken flower,
Wherein, I know, he loves, when evening comes,
To creep and lie all night, encanopied
Beneath the manifold and scented petals;
Fancying, he says, he bids the world adieu,
And is again a slumberer in heaven:
Or, in some other vein, perchance thou'lt find him
Within the halls or dens of some famed city.
Give thou a general search, in open day,
I'th' town and country's ample field; and next
Seek him in dusky cave, and in dim grot;
And in the shadow of the precipice,
Prone or supine extended motionless;
Or, in the twilight of o'erhanging leaves,
Swung at the nodding arm of some vast beech.
By moonlight seek him on the mountain, and
At noon in the translucent waters salt or fresh;
Or near the dank-marged fountain, or clear well,
Watching the tad-pole thrive on suck of venom;
Or where the brook runs o'er the stones, and smooths
Their green locks with its current's crystal comb.
Seek him in rising vapors, and in clouds
Crimson or dun; and often on the edge
Of the gray morning and of tawny eve:
Search in the rocky alcove and woody bower;
And in the crow's-nest look, and every
Pilgrim-crowd-drawing Idol, wherein he
Is wont to sit in darkness and be worshipped.

If thou shouldst find him not in these, search for him
By the lone melancholy tarns of bitterns;
And in the embosomed dells, whereunto maidens
Resort to bathe within the tepid pool.
Look specially there, and, if thou seest peeping
Satyr or faun, give chase and call out "Malzah!"
For he shall know thy voice and his own name.

EVENING SCENE.*

FROM THE BANKS OF THE DETROIT RIVER.

CHARLES SANGSTER.

I stood upon a bank that faced the West,
  Beyond me lay Lake Erie, softly calm,
Calm as the thoughts that soothe the dying breast
  As the Soul passes to the great I AM.

---

* We are disposed to think that any just estimate of MR. SANGSTER'S poetry will assign him the first place among Canadian poets. Others may have written as well and as sweetly on some themes as he could have done; but no one has contributed so largely to enrich Canadian poetry. No one has attempted so much. No one has displayed equal freshness and variety of imagery, in the treatment of national themes. Indeed, in the variety of subjects selected from the scenery, seasons, and past history of this country, and in the success and originality with which he has treated them, he has no competitor whatever. His genius is more truly Canadian than that of any other poet of distinction in this Province. Many other Canadian poets, having spent their youth in some other land, though cherishing a strong regard for the country of their adoption, keep their tenderest affection for the land of their birth; selecting their principal imagery and illustrations from its scenery and associations, somewhat to the neglect of the materials, which nature so profusely lavishes on the scenery of this country. But Mr. S., while cherishing a loyal attachment to the mother land, gives Canada the chief place in his heart. Her mighty lakes and rivers—her forests and hills—her history, religion, and laws—her homes and liberties—her brave sons and fair daughters—are all objects of his most

One solitary bird melodiously
 Trilled its sweet vesper from a grove of elm,
One solitary sail upon the sea
 Rested, unmindful of its potent helm.

There lay the Island with its sanded shore,
 The snow-white Lighthouse, like an Angel-friend
Dressed in his fairest robes, and evermore
 Guiding the mariner to some promised end.

And down behind the forest trees, the sun,
 Arrayed in burning splendors, slowly rolled,
Like to some sacrificial urn, o'errun
 With flaming hues of crimson, blue and gold.

And round about him, fold on fold, the clouds,
 Steeped in some rainbow essence, lightly fell,
Draped in the living glory that enshrouds
 His nightly entrance to his ocean shell.

---

ardent affection, graven alike upon the pages of his poetry, and upon the tablets of his heart. The most prominent characteristics of his genius are, a wonderful fertility of thought, which inables him to pour forth images, and forms of expression with lavish prodigality;—an intense sympathy with Nature, in all her varied moods and forms;—and that peculiar freshness and originality of language that is the sure distinction of those, to whom belong "the vision and the faculty divine." Occasionally, too, we catch glimpses of a philosophic spirit, capable of grappling with the deep problems of the world of mind. Mr. Sangster was born in Upper Canada, in 1822, and resides at Kingston. His whole life has been one hard battle with unpropitious circumstances; but he has held on his way with a brave and unflinching heart. His two volumes, "*The St. Lawrence and the Saguenay*," published in 1856, and "*Hesperus*," published in 1860, are rich in poetic power and beauty, though like all other ventures in Canadian poetry, they have not awakened interest, or secured patronage, at all proportionate to their merit.

The woods were flashing back his gorgeous light,
  The waters glowed beneath the varied green,
Ev'n to the softened shadows, all was bright,
  Heaven's smile was blending with the view terrene.

The lofty woods, in summer sheen arrayed,
  The trembling poplar with its silver leaf,
The stately walnut rising o'er the glade,
  The willow bending with its load of grief:

The graceful elm, the energetic oak,
  The red-leaved maple, and the slender pine,
The grove of firs, half hidden by the smoke
  From the white cottage clothed with jessamine;

The thirsty cattle drinking from the spring,
  Or standing mid-deep in the sunny stream,
The stream itself, like Joy, meandering,—
  A silver shaft shot down a golden beam:

The ruddy orchard with its tempting fruit,
  The juicy apple, and the mellow pear,
The downy peach, and near the garden, mute
  With eager visions of a fruitful share,

Lolled the young urchin on his bed of grass,
  Thinking of Autumn, with her red ripe-store—
So Boyhood smiles to mark the seasons pass,
  And Manhood sighs that they return no more:

On these the parting Day poured down a stream
  Of radiant, unimaginable light,
Like as in some celestial spirit-dream
  A thousand rainbows melt upon the sight,

Setting the calm horizon all ablaze
  With splendors stolen from the crypts of heaven,
Dissolving with their magic heat the maze
  Of clouds that nestle to the breast of even.

The fisher ceased his song, hung on his oars,
  Pausing to look, a pulse in every breath,
And, in imagination, saw the shores
  Elysian rising o'er the realms of Death.

And as he dreamed, the sunlight passed away,
  The stream gave back no deep cerulean hue,
Eve's purple finger closed the lips of Day,
  And a dim glory clothed the upper blue.

And down on tip-toe came the gradual Night,
  A gentle Twilight first, with silver wings,
And still from out the darkening infinite
  Came shadowy forms, like deep imaginings.

There was no light in all the brooding air,
  There was no darkness yet to blind the eyes,
But through the space interminable, there
  Nature and Silence passed in solemn guise.

THE WATCHER.

HELEN M. JOHNSON.

Night comes, but he comes not! I fear
The treacherous ice; what do I hear?
Bells? nay, I am deceived again,—
'Tis but the ringing in my brain.

—O how the wind goes shrieking past!
Was it a voice upon the blast?
A cry for aid? my God protect!
Preserve his life—his course direct!
—How suddenly it has grown dark—
How very dark without—hush! hark!
—'Tis but the creaking of the door;
It opens wide and nothing more.
Then wind and snow came in; I thought
Some straggler food and shelter sought;
But more I feared, for fear is weak,
That some one came of him to speak.
To tell how long he braved the storm,
How long he kept his bosom warm
With thoughts of home, how long he cheered
His weary horse that plunged, and reared,
And wallowed through the drifted snow
Till daylight faded, and the glow
Of hope went out; how almost blind,
He peered around, below, behind,—
No road, no track, the very shore
All blotted out,—one struggle more,
It is thy last, perchance, brave heart!
O God! a reef! the masses part
Of snow and ice, and dark and deep
The waters lie in death-like sleep;—
He sees too late the chasm yawn;
Sleigh, horse, and driver, all are gone!
Father in heaven! It may be thus,
But thou are gracious,—pity us.
Save him, and me in mercy spare
What 'twould be worse than death to bear.

—Hark! hark! am I deceived again?
Nay, 'tis no ringing in my brain,
My pulses leap—my bosom swells—
Thank God! it is, *it is his bells!*

THE SLEIGH-BELL.

JOHN F. M'DONNELL.

The eve is clear, and the golden light
Plays on the Winter's robe of white.
Smooth is the road on the dazzling snow,
Lightly the sleighs o'er the deep drifts go:—
Ours is a path as wild and free
As a bounding bark's on the stormy sea.
The sleigh-bells chime on the frosty air,
Like the voice of a spirit chanting there,
The joys of the Winter's festive hour,
Though it brings not fruit, nor blooming flower.
    Tinkle, tinkle!—the sleigh-bells' chime
        Mounts on the wings of the frosty air,
    Like the song of a bird of a summer clime,
        When the woods are green, and the sky is fair.

Over hill and plain, we swiftly glide,—
O'er the ice-bound river's foaming tide,
And deep in the vale where the dark pine trees
Shelter our path from the biting breeze.
The Eve is fading,—the pall of Night
Closeth the East from our straining sight,
And far in the West, a dying glow
Throws a crimson blush o'er the sea of snow

Then speed us on, for the sun is set;
Through the forest's gloom, we've a long way yet.
Tinkle, tinkle!—the sleigh bells' chime
Rings through the forest vales afar,
And from the dome of heaven's bright clime,
Glimmers the ray of the Evening Star.

O CAN YOU LEAVE YOUR NATIVE LAND?

(For Music.)

MRS. MOODIE.

O can you leave your native land,
An exile's bride to be;
Your mother's home and cheerful hearth
To tempt the main with me—
Across the wide and stormy sea
To trace our foaming track,
And know the wave that heaves us on
Will never bear us back?

And can you in Canadian wood
With me the harvest bind,
Nor feel one lingering sad regret
For all you leave behind!
Can those dear hands, unused to toil,
The woodman's wants supply,
Nor shrink beneath the chilly blast
When wintry storms are nigh?

Amid the shades of forests dark,
  Our loved isle will appear
An Eden, whose delicious bloom
  Will make the wild more drear—
And you in solitude will weep
  O'er scenes belov'd in vain,
And pine away your life to view
  Once more your native plain!

Then pause, dear girl, ere those fond lips
  Your wanderer's fate decide;
My spirit spurns the selfish wish—
  You must not be my bride—
But oh, that smile—those tearful eyes
  My firmer purpose move—
Our hearts are one—and we will dare
  All perils thus to love.

SONNET—WINTER NIGHT.

C. HEAVYSEGE.

The stars are setting in the frosty sky,
  Numerous as pebbles on a broad sea coast;
While o'er the vault the cloud-like galaxy
  Has marshalled its innumerable host.
Alive all heaven seems: with wondrous glow,
  Tenfold refulgent every star appears;
As if some wide, celestial gale did blow,
  And thrice illume the ever-kindled spheres.

Orbs, with glad orbs rejoicing, burning, beam
 Ray-crowned, with lambent lustre in their zones;
Till o'er the blue, bespangled spaces seem
 Angels and great archangels on their thrones;—
A host divine, whose eyes are sparkling gems,
 And forms more bright than diamond diadems.

WINTER IN CANADA.

MRS. J. L. LEPROHON.

Nay, tell me not that with shivering fear,
You shrink from the thought of wintering here;
That the cold intense of our winter time,
Is severe as that of Siberian clime;
And if wishes could waft across the sea,
To-night in your English home you would be.

Remember, no hedges there now are bright
With verdure, or blossoms of hawthorn white;
In damp sodden fields, or bare garden beds,
No daisies or cowslips show their fair heads;
Whilst cold chilling winds and skies of dark hue,
Tell, in England, as elsewhere, 'tis winter too.

Raise your eyes to our skies of azure hue,
Admire their gleaming, metallic blue,
Look round on the earth robed in bridal white,
All glittering and flashing with diamonds bright,
Whilst o'erhead, her lover and lord, the sun,
Shines brightly as e'er in Summer he's done.

In a graceful sleigh, drawn by spirited steed,
You glide o'er the snow with lightning speed,
Whilst from harness decked with silvery bells,
In sweet showers the sound on the clear air swells,
And the keen bracing breeze with vigor rife,
Sends quick through your veins warm streams of life.

On, with your snow-shoes, so strong and light,
Thick blanket-coat, sash of scarlet bright,
And away o'er the deep and untrodden snow,
Through wood, o'er mountain, untrammelled to go,
Through lone narrow paths where in years long fled,
The Indian passed with light active tread.

What! dare to rail at our snow storms—O why
Not view them with poet's or artist's eye,
Watch each pearly flake as it falls from above,
Like snowy plumes from some spotless dove,
Clothing all objects in ermine of air,
Far purer than that which monarchs wear!

Have you not witnessed our glorious nights,
So brilliant with gleaming Northern-lights,
Quick flashing and darting across the sky,
Whilst afar in the starry heavens high,
The shining moon pours down streams of light,
O'er the silent earth robed in dazzling white?

There are times, too, our woods show wondrous sights,
Such as are read of in "Arabian Nights,"
When branch and bough are all laden with gems,
And sparkle like Eastern diadems;
And the sun sheds a blaze of dazzling light,
On ruby, opal, and diamond bright.

But tarry till Spring on Canadian shore,
You'll rail at our winters then no more—
New health and fresh life through your veins shall glow,
Spite of piercing winds, spite of ice and snow,
And I'd venture to promise in truth my friend,
'Twill not be the last that with us you'll spend.

LAKE ERIE.

WILLIAM WYE SMITH.

I looked upon Lake Erie
   Before I looked on thee,
And I'll not leave it for thy gold
   That lies beyond the sea ;—
Its waves come leaping to my hand,
   As if they fear'd I'd go—
I look upon Lake Erie,
   And my heart gives answer no!"

Upon the shores of Erie,
   My cradle-song was sung;
And round its coves, and o'er its deeps
   My childish shoutings rung;—
Nor think my heart can e'er forget
   The old love and the true—
Upon the shores of Erie
   That round its magic threw.

Thou bid'st me seek some other land
   Away beyond the Line,
Where gold is like the river sand
   And spice grows like the pine—

I've heard it all—yet Canada
Has earned so well my love,
That when I seek some other land
'Twill be the land above!

ST. GEORGE'S FLAG.

MRS. FAULKNER.

St. George for merry England, ho! up with the pennon brave,
It hath streamed o'er many a conquered land, o'er many a distant wave;
Up with the Red-cross banner! 'tis a glorious sight to see,
The noblest flag that ever flew, stream out so fair and free.

It floated o'er proud Acre's towers in days long passed away,
When Lion Richard led his host at the holy tomb to pray;
And still the Crescent paler waned before the hallowed sign,
That flew in triumph o'er thy fields, oh! sacred Palestine.

It cheered Old England's stalwart sons thro' Cressy's hard won fray.
It waved o'er Royal Henry's head on Agincourt's proud day;
The sultry breath of sunny Spain its crimson cross has fanned,
And gallant hosts have borne it on through India's burning land.

Oh! many a flag of gaudier hue the fanning breeze may wave,
But none that bears a nobler name, more stainless or more brave;
None that hath led more dauntless hearts to battle for the right,
None that hath flown more proudly o'er the crimson field of fight.

Up with the brave old banner then, the peerless and the bold,
True hearts will rally round it yet as in the days of old;
And still on every English lip the thrilling cry shall be
St. George for merry England, ho! God and our own country.

ON-TA-RI-O.

J. GEORGE HODGINS.

On-ta-ri-o, On-ta-ri-o,
  How bright thy waters flow!
How joyously they dance along;
  How music-like they go!
The Western wilds have heard thy song—
  Have sighed thy passing thence;
With joy old Ocean's bosom swells
  To greet thy coming hence!

On-ta-ri-o, On-ta-ri-o,
  Thou beauteous mimic sea!
Thine entrance here,* how grand—sublime—
  How dashing, wild, and free!
A thousand anthems tuned their voice,
  A thousand thunders rolled,
As on thy surge-like billows swelled
  In burnished sheets of gold!

O'er thee, ere white man's foot had pressed
  Thy banks of verdant green,
Or on thy bounding billows, wide,
  The whitened sail was seen,

---

* At Niagara.

The sun's bright rays of golden tinge
  Fell on the frail canoe,
Which bore the Sovereign of these glades
  Swift o'er thy waters blue!

Along thy banks, while in his pride,
  The red man's dance and song
In savage triumph—stern and wild—
  Rose from each victor-throng,
In proud defiance to their foes,
  Through the green forests rung,
Or keenest anguish—tearless grief—
  Their stoic bosoms stung.

But where are *now* thy dusky chiefs;
  That haughty warrior-band,
Who long a mighty sceptre swayed
  O'er all this forest land?
Where are those dauntless spirits now:
  Those heroes of the past?
And where is proud *Toronto* † gone,
  Thy bravest and thy *last?*

From thy dark caves no answer flows,
  No hushed response is borne,
Save the low murmur of thy waves
  As they unceasing mourn,
And ever chant a dirge-like strain—
  A solemn requiem slow—
For Chiefs, who ever fearless met,
  Nor blanched before the foe!

---

† Tradition gives the name of *Toronto* as that of a noted Indian chief in the vicinity of the Lake.

They're gone! bright Lake! yet *still*, in pride,
  Thy dark blue waters flow,
As when thy free-born forest-sons
  First drew the hunter's bow;
And now, far o'er thy glittering wave
  And billowy crest of snow,
The *Star* and *Meteor* banners float;
  Thou'rt still On-ta-ri-o!

I'VE WANDERED IN THE SUNNY SOUTH.

NATIONAL SONG.

JOHN F. M'DONNELL.

I've wandered in the sunny South,
  Beneath its purple skies;
And roamed through many a far-off land,
  Where cloudless beauty lies:
I've breathed the balm of tropic eves,
  Upon the Southern sea;
And watched the glorious sunset pour
  Its radiance far and free.

But give me still my Northern home,—
  Her islands and her lakes;
And her forests old, where not a sound
  The tomb-like silence breaks.
More lovely in her snowy dress,
  Or in her vesture green,
Than all the pride of Europe's lands,
  Or Asia's glittering sheen.

I've basked beneath Italian suns,
  When flowers were in their bloom;
And I've wandered o'er the hills of Greece,
  By ruined shrine and tomb;—
Oh sweet it was to gaze upon
  The Arno's silver tide—
And dearer still, the ruins grey
  Of Athen's fallen pride.

But dearer unto me that land
  Which the mighty waters lave,
Where the spreading maple's glorious hues
  Are mirrored in the wave:—
Where music from the dark old woods
  Ascends to heaven's dome—
Like angel hymns of peace and love—
  Around my Northern home.

THE EMBLEMS OF OUR HOMES.

ROBERT STUART PATTERSON.

O blessed and free Britannia,
  The mistress of the deep,
Around whose shores the subject waves
  A watchful vigil keep,—
The LION crouching by thy side
  Is not more nobly brave
Than thy soldiers in the battle,
  Thy sailors on the wave.

Thy emblem flower is fairest
 Of all the Floral band;
But lovelier than Roses
 Are the daughters of thy Land.

O best beloved Hibernia,
 Thou Emerald-gemmèd Queen,
With crown of wreathed "*Arbutus*"
 And "*triple leaf*" of green,—
The hearts are ever warm and true,
 And ever bright the smile
Of the manly sons and blue-eyed maids,
 The children of thine isle.

O sternly beauteous Scotia,
 The land of hill and glen,
The land of lochs and mountain streams,
 The home of warlike men;
The thorn-girt Thistle on thy crest
 Is as the groves of spears
And claymores bright, in the trusty grasp
 Of thy hardy Mountaineers.

O snow and pine clad Canada,
 Old England's loyal child,
With inland lakes like oceans,
 With forests dark and wild,
With the fall of thy Niagara
 Loud as a rushing sea,
The Beaver and the Maple Leaf
 Thy emblems still shall be.

Oh monarch never wore a crown
  So richly fair I ween,
As a garland with such emblems formed
  To deck our noble Queen.

HOW THEY DIED AT THANSI.*

MISS MURRAY.

O Scotland! mother of brave men,
  Who battled for the right,
Whose glory gilds thy wildest glen
  And sternest mountain height,
And shines o'er many a distant land,
  Where Scottish lays proclaim
The worth of that immortal band,
  Which thou hast given to fame.

Men of free thought and lofty deed,
  Firm, steadfast, strong and true,
Who never in the hour of need
  A craven terror knew,
For liberty and thee they fought,
  They struggled, suffered, died;
And left the noble deeds they wrought
  To crown thy brows with pride.

---

*MISS MURRAY, though not extensively known as a poet, is a lady of rare intellectual gifts, and has won a high reputation in prose-fiction. Her productions in this department of literature will compare favourably with those of the most eminent writers of the day. "THE CITED CURATE," recently concluded in the "*British American Magazine*," evinces more genuine intellectual power than any similar production we have seen from a Canadian pen.

A proud, glad mother should'st thou be,
  For still each gallant son
That glory safely guards for thee
  Their elder brothers won.
The free and fearless blood that flamed
  Of old in Scottish veins,
By no fierce tyrant ever tamed,
  Its ancient fire retains.

Not theirs the limbs that fly or yield;
  That dauntless hardihood,
Which once on Bannockburn's red field
  An English host withstood,
Held firm on that Crimean plain,
  Where Russian horse assailed
Brave Campbell's iron men in vain—
  In valor triple-mailed.

Still these fought by their comrades' side
  Against an equal foe,
With all those aids to manly pride
  Brothers-in-arms bestow.
But he whose sad heroic fate
  Thrills all who hear it told;
Whose death in grandeur well may mate
  Some hero's death of old,—

A hopeless strife could calmly dare
  With one slight hand to aid,
One tender woman's heart to share
  The gallant stand he made.

And bravely did she bear her part,
  What woman ever fails
When love has strung and nerved her heart?
  Love over death prevails.

But there are evils worse than death!
  Insult and outrage dread,
The writhing, yelling fiends beneath
  May wreak upon her head:
"No, never! we know how to die!"
  He turned to her, and caught
A radiant flash from her bright eye,
  That answered to his thought.

"Yes! let us die, unsullied, free,
  O Father hear our cry!
Save these two souls that trust in thee,—
  To thee for refuge fly!"
He kissed her with a fonder kiss,
  A truer, nobler pride,
Than ever in hours of peaceful bliss
  A bridegroom kissed his bride.

"True heart! so tender and so brave,
  My faithful, loving wife,
This hand, though powerless now to save,
  Still guards thy better life.
Our souls shall find a home in heaven;
  My rifle still rings true;
I murmur not, since God has given
  A brave death shared with you!"

In his firm hand his rifle good
Had failed not once that day.
Its dreaded aim that demon brood
Still kept at furious bay.
It failed not now—without a pang
Her pure brave spirit fled.
Again th' unerring bullet rang—
He too had joined the dead.

Give honor to those noble hearts;
Bravely and well they died;
The tear that to their memory starts
In proud content is dried.
With Scotland's bravest and her best
She'll give them place, I ween,
And deep within her granite breast
She'll grave the name of Skene!

When the Indian insurrection broke out at Thansi, Captain Alexander Skene and his wife took refuge in a tower, and made a brave and protracted defence. Mrs. Skene loaded her husband's rifles, and he fired till he had shot thirty-seven of the rebels; when finding it impossible to keep them out any longer, he kissed his wi fe, shot her, and then shot himself.

EVENING.

HELEN M. JOHNSON.

It is a lovely scene; the sun has set,
But left his glory in the western sky,
Where daylight lingers, half regretful yet
That sombre Night, her sister, draweth nigh,
And one pale star just looketh from on high;

'Tis neither day nor night, but both have blent
Their own peculiar charms to please the eye,—
Declining day its sultry heat has spent,
And calm refreshing night its grateful freshness lent.
The lake is sleeping—on its quiet breast
Are clouds of every tint the rainbows wear,
Some are in crimson, some in gold are dressed.
Oh had I wings, like yonder birds of air,
How I would love to dip my pinions there,
Then mount exulting to the heavenly gate,—
A song of love and gratitude to bear
To Him who gives the lovely and the great,
In earth and sea and sky, so glorious an estate.

It is the time when angels are abroad
Upon their work of love and peace to men,—
Commissioned from the dazzling throne of God,
They come to earth as joyfully as when
The tidings ran o'er mountain and o'er glen,
"A Son is born, a Saviour and a King,"—
For they have tidings glorious as then,
Since tokens from our risen Lord they bring,
That life has been secured, and death has lost its sting.

The twilight deepens; o'er the distant hill
A veil is spread of soft and misty grey;
And from the lake so beautiful and still,
The images of sunset fade away;
The twinkling stars come forth in bright array,
Which shunned the splendor of the noontide glare,—
A holy calm succeeds the bustling day,
And gentle voices, stealing through the air,
Proclaim to hearts subdued the hour for grateful prayer.

THE CANADIAN HERD-BOY.

(A Song of the Backwoods.)

MRS. MOODIE.

Through the deep woods, at peep of day,
The careless herd-boy wends his way,
By piny ridge and forest stream,
To summon home his roving team—
Cobos! cobos! from distant dell
Sly echo wafts the cattle bell.

A blythe reply he whistles back,
And follows out the devious track,
O'er fallen tree and mossy stone,
A path to all save him unknown—
Cobos! cobos! far down the dell,
More faintly falls the cattle bell.

See the dark swamp before him throws
A tangled maze of cedar boughs,
On all around deep silence broods,
In nature's boundless solitudes—
Cobos! cobos! the breezes swell,
As nearer floats the cattle bell.

He sees them now—beneath yon trees
His motley herd recline at ease;
With lazy pace and sullen stare
They slowly leave their shady lair—
Cobos! cobos! far up the dell
Quick jingling comes the cattle bell.

THE OLD SUGAR CAMP.

HELEN M. JOHNSON.

Come let us away to the old Sugar Camp;
The sky is serene though the ground may be damp,—
And the little bright streams, as they frolic and run,
Turn a look full of thanks to the ice-melting sun;
While the warm southern winds, wherever they go,
Leave patches of brown 'mid the glittering snow.

The oxen are ready, and Carlo and Tray
Are watching us, ready to be on the way,
While a group of gay children with platter and spoon,
And faces as bright as the roses of June,
O'er fences and ditches exultingly spring,
Light-hearted and careless as birds on the wing.

Where's Edwin? O here he comes loading his gun;
Look out for the partridges—hush! there is one!
Poor victim! a bang and a flutter—'tis o'er,—
And those fair dappled wings shall expand nevermore;
It was shot for our invalid sister at home,
Yet we sigh as beneath the tall branches we roam.

Our cheeks all aglow with the long morning tramp,
We soon come in sight of the old Sugar Camp;
The syrup already is placed in the pan,
And we gather around it as many as can,—
We try it on snow, when we find it is done,
We will fill up a mould for a dear absent one.

O, gayest and best of all parties are these,
That meet in the Camp 'neath the old maple trees,
Renewing the love and the friendship of years,—
They are scenes to be thought of with smiles and with tears,
When age shall have furrowed each beautiful cheek,
And left in dark tresses a silvery streak.

Here brothers and sisters and lovers have met,
And cousins and friends we can never forget;
The prairie, the ocean divide us from some,
Yet oft as the seasons for sugaring come,
The cup of bright syrup to friendship we'll drain,
And gather them home to our bosoms again.

Dear Maple, that yieldeth a nectar so rare,
So useful in spring and in summer so fair,—
Of autumn acknowledged the glory and queen,
Attendant on every Canadian scene,
Enshrined in our homes, it is meet thou should'st be
Of our country the emblem, O beautiful Tree!

THE VOYAGEUR'S SONG.

JOHN F. M'DONNELL.

We track the herds o'er the prairies wide,
  Through the length of the summer day;
And guide the canoe on the rapid's tide,
  Where the waters flash in the ray;
Where the silvery scales of the salmon glance
  On the bosom of the pool:—

And we rest our wearied limbs at eve,
  In the shade of the pine-trees cool.
Let others toil for golden store;
  For riches little we care:
    Oh, the happiest life
    In this world of strife,
  Is that of a Voyageur.

When the red sun sinks in the golden West,
  At evening when he goes
With ministering hosts of the golden clouds,
  To seek the night's repose—
We pitch our tents on the soft green sward,—
  And we light our evening fire,—
And we mingle strains of our Northern land
  With the notes of the forest choir.
Time flies along, with jest and song,
  For our merry men are there:
    Oh there's not a life,
    In this world of strife,
  Like that of a Voyageur.

O sweet and soft are our couches made,
  With the broad green summer leaves,
And the curtains spread above the head
  Are those which Nature weaves.
The tall oak and the spreading elm
  Are twined in a tangled screen,—
Surpassing far all the magic skill
  Of the sculptor's art e'er seen.

We shun the noise of the busy world,
  For there's crime and misery there;
    And the happiest life,
    In this world of strife,
  Is that of a Voyageur.

ADDRESS TO THE RIVER GARNOCK.

(*From the "Moorland Minstrel."*)

THOMAS M'QUEEN.

Oft, Garnock, oft in this lone spot,
  In boyhood's brighter day,
With feelings ne'er to be forgot,
I marked thy waters onward float—
  Wave after wave away.

And I was young—and on this brow
  Grief ventured not to trace
Those furrows that becloud it now;
Nor had my young soul learned to bow
  Beneath the world's disgrace.

And I marvelled much, as speedily
  Thy dark waves floated on,
What length and breadth had floated by—
Whence wast thou—whither went'st—and why
  Thy waters ne'er were done.

But years on years have sped away,
  And in their devious course
Have blent my auburn locks with gray,
And scattered wrinkles and decay,
  And tremblings of remorse.

The sacred ties of life's young day
  Were long since forced to sever,
And the holy sounds of love's sweet lay,
Youth's melody and mirth so gay,
  Are silent now forever.

Less lovely Spring's green robes appear,—
  Less bright the moon's pale beam,
The summer's sun looks dull and drear,
And the former charms of Nature wear
  The semblance of a dream.

The lightsome heart—the laughing eye—
  The hope that lured me on—
The voice that sung my lullaby,
And the youthful peers that shared my joy—
  These all are dead and gone.

The budding spring—the blooming May—
  The blackbird's soothing strain—
The schoolboy's gambols on the way,
But bring to mind a happier day,
  That cannot come again.

I've drank the common cup of woe
  From Friendship's frozen hand;
I've wandered heartless to and fro,
And suffered pangs that none can know,
  'Mid simpering follies bland.

Again I come—but changed in all
  Save the unborrowed name,
To list the once-loved waterfall
Pour forth its midnight madrigal,
  Eternally the same.

No change has come on thee—the years
  That fleetly have gone by,
And mingled sorrows, sighs, and tears,
And blighted hopes and fostered fears,
  Have failed to drain thee dry.

Ages elapsed have seen thee glide,
  Thou lonely moorland river;
Yet on thy undiminished tide,
Wave after wave thy bubbles ride
  Majestical as ever.

In pyramid, or tower or tomb,
  Man struggles to obtain
Reversion of the dreaded doom,
Of being lost in time to come;
  But, ah! the hope is vain.

Yon tower, of rude, unchartered day,
  That frowns above thy stream,
In crumbling atoms seems to say:—
"*Man and his labours pass away*
  Unheeded as a dream."

And thou wert ere Glengarnock's wall
  Had reared its feudal head;
Thou saw'st the glories of its hall,
Thou sing'st the requiem of its fall,
  When countless years have fled.

Yea, thou wert ere frail fleeting man
  Earth's flowery surface trode,
Thou saw'st him first presume to scan,
And reason falsely from a plan
  That told him of a God.

Thou saw'st his Druid altars dyed
  With blood of burning men;
With bow and quiver by his side,
He ranged for prey the forest wide,
  The mountain and the glen.

He changed his painted skin and hair,
  His creed and sacrifice—
And, humming through the woods of Blair
Thou heard'st Saint Winning's evening prayer
  To countless deities.

Thou seest him still the child of change,
  Nor less the child of thrall,
Abjuring Nature's healthy range
For prison-toil and commerce strange,
  With scarce a God at all.

And yet thou art unchanged; the flood
  Hath foamed and fled away,
Leaving thy calm and native mood
To sing to hill and vale and wood,
  Thy philosophic lay.

Down, down to ocean's dread abyss
  Thy waters, as of yore,
In endless waves successive press;
Yet, strange! thy stream grows nothing less,
  Nor grows the ocean more.

Roll on, thou liquid glassy sheet;
Roll on, methinks I see,
In thy unbroken waters fleet,
A sign, a pledge, an emblem meet,
Of immortality.

My toil-worn frame, like thine may seem,
Fast sinking to decay;
My life, my spirit, like thy stream,
Lit up at heaven's unfading beam,
Must glow and glow for aye.

Glide on, thou moorland river—roll
Thy dark waves to the sea—
So speeds my fleeting, deathless soul,
To some far, strange, mysterious goal
In vast eternity.

Miscellaneous Pieces.

HEROES!

ALEX. M'LACHLAN.

All hail to the chiefs of thought,
Who wield the mighty pen!
That light may at last be brought
To the darkened souls of men.
To the gifted seers who preach—
To the humble bards who sing;
To all the heads that teach
In truth's enchanted ring;

To the soldiers of the right—
  To the heroes of the true;
Oh! ours were a sorry plight,
  Great conquerors, but for you!
O ye are the men of worth!
  O ye are the men of might!
O ye are the kings of earth,
  And your swords are love and right.

'Tis not at the beat of drum,
  Earth's great ones do appear;
At the nation's call they come,
  But not with the sword or spear.
Then hail to the brave who lead
  In the humble paths of peace!
To the hearts that toil and bleed,
  That wrong may the sooner cease!

O what are the robes we wear,
  Or the heights to which we climb!
'Tis only the hearts we bear
  Can make our lives sublime.
'Tis only the good we do,
  That lives throughout all time;
'Tis only the faithful few
  Who reach the height sublime.

Then hail to the chiefs of thought,
  Who wield the mighty pen!
That light may at last be brought
  To the darken'd soul of men!

To the soldiers of the right—
  To the heroes of the true;
Oh! ours were a sorry plight,
  Great conquerors, but for you!

THE NIGHT COMETH.

ANNIE L. WALKER.

Work! for the night is coming;
  Work! through the morning hours;
Work! while the dew is sparkling;
  Work! 'mid the springing flowers;
Work! while the day grows brighter,
  Under the glowing sun;
Work! for the night is coming,
  Night—when man's work is done.

Work! for the night is coming;
  Work! through the sunny noon,
Fill the bright hours with labor;
  Rest cometh sure and soon.
Give to each flying minute
  Something to keep in store;
Work! for the night is coming;
  Night—when man works no more.

Work! for the night is coming;
  Under the sunset skies,
While their bright tints are glowing,
  Work! for the daylight flies.

Work ! till the last beam fadeth,
  Fadeth to shine no more ;—
Work while the night is darkening,—
  Night, when man's work is o'er.

COLIN.

CHARLES SANGSTER.

Who'll dive for the dead men now,
    Since Colin is gone ?
Who'll feel for the anguished brow,
    Since Colin is gone ?
True Feeling is not confined
To the learned or lordly mind ;
Nor can it be bought and sold
In exchange for an Alp of gold ;
For Nature, that never lies,
Flings back with indignant scorn
The counterfeit deed, still-born,
In the face of the seeming wise,
In the Janus face of the huckster race
Who barter her truths for lies.

Who'll wrestle with danger dire,
    Since Colin is gone ?
Who'll fearlessly brave the maniac wave,
Thoughtless of self, human life to save,
Unmoved by the storm-fiend's ire ?
Who, Shadrach-like, will walk through fire,
    Since Colin is gone ?

Or hang his life on so frail a breath
That there's but a step 'twixt life and death?
For courage is not the heritage
Of the nobly born; and many a sage
Has climbed to the temple of fame,
And written his deathless name
In letters of golden flame,
Who' on glancing down
From his high renown,
Saw his unlettered sire
Still by the old log fire,
Saw the unpolished dame—
And the hovel from which he came.

Ah, ye who judge the dead
By the outward lives they led,
And not by the hidden worth
Which none but God can see;
Ye who would spurn the earth
That covers such as he;
Would ye but bear your hearts,
Cease to play borrowed parts,
And come down from your self-built throne:
How few from their house of glass,
As the gibbering secrets pass,
Would dare to fling, whether serf or king,
The first accusing stone!

Peace, peace to his harmless dust!
    Since Colin is gone;
We can but hope and trust;
Man judgeth, but God is just;
    Poor Colin is gone!

Had he faults? His heart was true,
And warm as the summer's sun.
Had he failings? Ay, but few;
'Twas an honest race he run.
Let him rest in the poor man's grave,
Ye who grant him no higher goal;
There may be a curse on the hands that gave,
But not on his simple soul!

UNSELFISH LOVE.

REV. J. A. ALLEN.

Love, like verdant spring,
Bright, beautiful thing,
  Steps forth from the winter of self;
Yet, like the fair dawn
On the poor man's lawn,
  Is too rich to be purchased by pelf.

Pure love, like the root,
Exists for the fruit,
  Content to lie hid from our view,
Beneath the cold sod:
The image of God,
  Who, pervading all things through and through,

Works ever the same,
Unheeding of blame
  Or praise—like the stillness of night—
In the untrodden waste,
And provinces vast
  And peopled concealed from all sight.

Pure love is the flower
That laughs when clouds lower,
  Expecting the soft vernal rains
To ripen the seed,
But takes little heed
  Of the ills her own beauty sustains:

Or like the fair star,
That shineth from far,
  When all things are buried in night;
But when the bright day,
With worthier ray,
  Robes nature in vesture of light,

So gently retires,
Till darkness requires
  Her aid, when she noiselessly steals
Once more to her post
Of duty, and lost
  To all selfish interest, feels

The pure joy of love;
But soon as, above
  The sky verge, orbed Luna is seen,
She leaves night so fair,
As best, to her care,
  And retires to the blue depths serene.

A VOICE FOR THE TIMES.

JENNIE E. HAIGHT.

Raise the hammer, strike the anvil,
  Let the wide earth feel the blow;
Let her quake from zone to centre,
  Tropic, vale, and peak of snow.

RIGHT, with sword drawn for the contest,
  Takes the field against the WRONG—
Sound aloud the deep-toned clarion,
  Let its notes be clear and long.

Human hearts with anguish bleeding,
  Human nature, held in thrall,
Myriads, waiting for redemption,
  Marshal at the trumpet's call.
Hold aloft your glorious banner,
  Let it float against the sky,
And with TRUTH's bright sword uplifted,
  Vow to conquer, though ye die.

Let no heart quail in the onset—
  From above, around, beneath,
Countless eyes the strife are watching,
  Through the war-cloud's dusky wreath,
Side by side all firm and valiant,
  In the God of Battles strong,
Grapple with each rampant error,
  In the serried ranks of WRONG.

Though the clouds, with thunder laden,
  Darken o'er the source of day—
Though the fork'd and fiery lightnings
  Flash and dart around your way;—
Echoed loud above the thunder
  Let your watchword, 'Victory,' sound;
And, amid the jagged lightnings,
  Inch by inch maintain your ground.

Where intrenched in hoary bulwarks,
  Error and his chieftains dwell,
Scale the rampart, strike the ensign;
  Track them to the gates of hell.
Not till then the waiting scabbard
  May receive the glitt'ring steel;
Not till then, earth's groaning millions
  Freedom's bounding pulse may feel.

On the distant, dim horizon,
  Faintly glim'ring through the night,
Shines a star whose noon-tide glory
  Truth's triumphal march shall light;
And e'en now, in far-off murm'rings
  O'er the future's restless sea,
Faith may catch a premonition
  Of the world's great jubilee.

THE STUDENT.

(*From Song of Charity.*)

E. J. CHAPMAN.

  How quiet is the antique room,
How darkening in the deepening gloom;
How quiet the dreamer dreaming there—
The floweret still in his hand,
That has led his thoughts all unaware
Into the far dream-land.
The twilight-gloom steals on apace;
But a windowed door on the garden looks,
And lets in light enough to shew

The calm sad smile on the dreamer's face;
And the walls of the room all dark with books,
And, piled against the sides below,
Huge coral-forms, and strange-life things.
Awakening up imaginings
Of palm-isles set in a tropic sea.
And at the back, a glittering store
Of instruments. Rare balances,
And lamps, and flasks, and furnaces,
By which men win the golden lore
Time-fruited from old alchemy.
And heaped around on shelf and floor,
Shells rock-entombed, and shining ore,
And mammoth-tooth, and saurian-bone;
And many a dull discolored stone,
The use of which she cannot see—
The good old servant, Margery!

Already on his brow and face
Had time and suffering left their trace;
But in his eyes, and in his smile,
The light of youth yet lived a while.
And the rare freshness of the days gone by
Still kept his heart full faithfully:
Although, amidst the living green,
Long-withered hopes that once had been
Life's holiest spells all thickly clung—
For he had loved when life was young,
With all the pure deep faith of Youth,
With all that heart's strong simple truth:
Loved!—and for two soul-garnered years
He lived as though the world had not
Upon its face a single spot

That ever had known a stain of tears.
Then the dream broke: and blackness fell
Over his life; for she—ah well,
The world is full of it: 'twas nothing new—
She changed—and soon between the two
There stood a barrier like the grave!

Thus passed the promise that his young life gave,
And he was left hope-wrecked and desolate
To struggle with his weary fate;
And with a white-robed ghost, that ever,
With thick fair hair and violet eyes,
Stood by his soul, but gave replies
To his passionate breathings—never!
Yet he would not, would not part
With those old memories of his heart,
For all the weary ache they brought it:
They kept its fount of kindness free,
A fount of flowing sympathy,
For other hope-wrecked hearts that sought it.

THE APPLE WOMAN.*

GEO. MARTIN.

She often comes, a not unwelcome guest,
With her old face set in a marble smile,
And bonnet ribbonless—it is her best,
And little cloak—and blesses you the while,

---

* Mr. Martin has been for some years, a contributor to the Montreal Press. He possesses a vigorous and original imagination: but the degiee of time and attention he has given to Poesie, has been too limited to enable him to do justice to his natural talents.

And cracks her joke, ambitious to beguile
Your heart to something human,
Then sets her basket down—a little rest!
The Apple Woman.

Her stock in trade that basket doth contain;
It is her wholesale and her retail store,
Her goods, and chattels,—all that doth pertain
To her estate, a daughter of the Poor;
O ye who tread upon a velvet floor,
Whose walls rich lights illumine,
Wound not with word or look of high disdain
The Apple Woman.

She is thy sister, jewelled Lady Clare,
"My sister! fling this insult in my face?"
How dare you then, when in the house of prayer,
Utter, "Our Father?" the difference of place
Nulls not the consanguinity of race,
And every creature human
Is kin to that poor mother, shivering there,
The Apple Woman.

She sits upon the side-walk in the cold,
And with her scraggy hand, hard-shrunk and blue,
And corded with the cordage of the old,
She reaches forth a *fameuse*, sir, to you,
And begs her ladyship will take one too,
And if you are a true man
Your pence will out; she never thinks of *gold*,
The Apple Woman.

She tells me—and I know she tells me true,
"My Good man,—God be kind!—had long been sick,
And one cold morning when the snow storm blew,
He said, Dear Bess, it grieves me to the quick
To see you venture out,—give me my stick,
I'll come to you at gloamin,
And bide you home,"—she paused, the rest I knew,
Poor Apple Woman.

Behold her then, a type of all that's good,
Honest in poverty, in suffering kind;
And large must be that love which strains for food,
Through wind and rain, through frost and snows that
For a sick burden that is left behind: [blind,
Call her but common;
God's commonest things are little understood,
Poor Apple Woman.

Two April weeks, I missed her, only two,
Missed her upon the side-walk, everywhere,
And when again she chanced to cross my view,
The marble smile was changed, it still was there,
But darkly veined, an emblem of despair;
A God-knit union
Grim death had struck, whose dark shock shivered through
The Apple Woman.

A widow now, she tells the bitter tale,
Tells how she sat within their little room
In yon dark alley, till she saw him fail,
Sat all alone through night's oppressive gloom,
Sat by her Joe as in a desert tomb,

No candle to illumine
His cold dead face! God only heard her wail,
Poor Apple Woman!

Now, when you meet her of the Basket-Store,
Her of the little cloak and bonnet bare,
Reach forth a friendly hand and something more,
When your portemonnaie has a coin to spare.
Dear are the hopes that mitigate thy care,
Dear the unbought communion
Whose tall vine reaches to the golden shore,
Poor Apple Woman!

MEMORY BELLS.

PAMELIA S. VINING.

Up from the spirit-depth ringing,
Softly your melody swells,
Sweet as a seraphim's singing,
Tender-toned, memory bells!
The laughter of childhood,
The song of the wildwood,
The tinkling of streams through the echoing dell;
The voice of a mother,
The shout of a brother,
Up from life's morning melodiously swell.

Up from the spirit-depths ringing,
Richly your melody swells,
Sweet reminiscences bringing,
Joyous-toned memory bells!

Youth's beautiful bowers,
Her dew-spangled flowers,
The pictures which Hope of futurity drew;
Love's rapturous vision
Of regions elysian,
In glowing perspective unfolding to view.

Up from the spirit-depths ringing,
Sadly your melody swells,
Tears with its mournful tones bringing,
Sorrowful memory bells!
The first heart-link broken,
The first farewell spoken,
The first flow'ret crushed in life's desolate track;
The agonized yearning
O'er joys unreturning,
All, all, with your low, wailing music come back.

Up from the spirit-depths ringing,
Dirge-like your melody swells;
But Hope wipes the tears that are springing,—
Mournful-toned memory bells!—
Above your deep knelling,
Her soft voice is swelling,
Sweeter than Angel-tones silvery clear!
Singing: in Heaven above,
All is unchanging love,
Mourner, look upward, thy home is not here!

O FOR AN HOUR OF CHILHOOD!

SAMUEL PAYNE FORD.

O for an hour of childhood!
One of those golden hours
When life was bright with sunshine,
And garlanded with flowers;
Ere the happy family circle,
That sat by the old stone hearth,
Was tearfully torn asunder
And scattered about the earth.

Could my childish wish be granted,
And Time turn back in his flight;
Which one of those hours of gladness
Would I have return to-night?
They are all of glad remembrance,
Though a few are dimmed with tears;
Say, which of those precious moments
Shall I call from the mist of years?

Shall I ask for the festal evening,
When father, and mother, and all
Were gathered together rejoicing
In the crowded Christmas hall?
And the gay, glad hours flew speedily,
With music and mirth, and chat?
Ah, no! for I see in the distance
A pleasanter hour than that.

Shall I ask for a summer morning,
When the birds are singing of love,
With never a cloud to darken
The bright blue sky above?
And trip with my little sister
All over the verdant lawn,
Plucking the flowers that blossom
As day begins to dawn;
And then spring cheerily forward
To the top of the pine-clad hill,
To see the sun rise in his beauty?
There are happier moments still.

Shall I ask for a time so often
Enjoyed in the "long ago,"
When after an hour's careering
So merrily over the snow,
An army of laughing loved ones,
All happy, and merry and strong,
We cheerfully tuned our voices
And joined in some sweet old song?
O! passing pleasant those hours were,
Nor shadowed by one regret,
Still ever there cometh the memory
Of holier moments yet.

May I have but one hour only?
I would have one most like heaven,
One calm, sweet hour, with all at home
On some quiet, Sabbath even?
Would list again to the voice of prayer
From hearts to God devoted,

And join again in the songs of praise
  That round the old rooms floated?
Would kneel again at my mother's knee,
  Beneath her smile of light,
And fall asleep with her lips on mine,
  Kissing a fond "good-night"?

WHERE'ER WE MAY WANDER.

ALEX. M'LACHLAN.

Where'er we may wander,
  Whate'er be our lot,
The heart's first affections
  Still cling to the spot
Where first a fond mother
  With rapture has prest,
Or sung us to slumber,
  In peace on her breast.

Where love first allured us,
  And fondly we hung
On the magical music
  Which fell from her tongue,
Tho' wise ones may tell us,
  'Twas foolish and vain,
Yet when shall we drink of
  Such glory again?

Where hope first beguiled us,
  And spells o'er us cast,
And told us her visions
  Of beauty would last,

That earth was an Eden,
  Untainted with guile,
And men were not destined
  To sorrow and toil.

Where friendship first found us,
  And gave us her hand,
And linked us for aye, to
  That beautiful band.
Oh still shall this heart be
  And cold as the clay,
Ere one of their features
  Shall from it decay.

O Fortune, thy favors
  Are empty and vain,
Restore me the friends of
  My boyhood again,
The hearts that are scattered,
  Or cold in the tomb,
O give me again, in
  Their beauty and bloom.

Tho' green are my laurels,
  And fresh is my fame,
And sweet is the magic
  Which dwells in a name,
How gladly I'd give them,
  To grasp but the hand
Of her that's away to
  The shadowy land.

Away with ambition,
  It brought me but pain;

O give me the big heart
  Of boyhood again.
The faith and the friendship,
  The rapture of yore,—
O shall they revisit
  This bosom no more?

GOOD-NIGHT.

HELEN M. JOHNSON.

Mother, good-night! my work is done,—
I go to rest with the setting sun;
But not to wake with the morning light,
So dearest mother, a long good-night!

Father, good-night! the shadows glide
Silently down to the river's side,
The river itself with stars is bright,
So dearest father, a long good-night!

Sister, good-night! the roses close
Their dewy eyes for the night's repose,—
And a strange damp mist obscures my sight,
So dearest sister, a long good-night!

Brother, good-night! the sunset flush
Has died away, and a midnight hush
Has settled o'er plain and mountain height,
So dearest brother, a long good-night!

Good-night! good-night! nay, do not weep;
I am weary of earth, I long to sleep;
I shall wake again with the dawning light
Of eternal day—good-night! good-night!

DREAMS.*

MRS. RHODA A. FAULKNER.

Dreams, mystic dreams, whence do ye come?
In what far land is your fairy home?
From whence at night do ye hither stray?
Where do ye flee at the dawn of day?
Ye never can fold your wand'ring wings,
Ye wild, unfathomable things.

Come ye from a beautiful world afar?
The land where the lost and the loved ones are,
That ye bring back so oft, in your shadowy reign,
The sound of their voices to earth again,
And their sunny smiles, and their looks of light,
In the silent hours of the quiet night.

Ye have brought again to the mother's breast
The child she hath laid in his grave to rest,
And she hears him prattling at her knee,
And she watches with joy his infant glee,

---

* The selections from MRS. FAULKNER in this collection, disclose the true spirit of poetry. They are taken from a little work, entitled "*Wild Notes from the Back Woods*," by R. A. P. (Rhoda Ann Page,) published in pamphlet form at Cobourg, in 1850. During the compilation of these "selections," we wrote to Mrs. Faulkner for some contributions for the work. Her husband replied, stating that, through severe illness, she was unable, for the present, to comply with this request. A few weeks after, "*Wild Notes*" was sent to the editor, by Dr. Powell of Cobourg, with a request to insert some pieces from it in this work, and stating at the same time that the author had died the week before. We feel, therefore, a melancholy pleasure in preserving a few of her poems in a more permanent form, and introducing them to a wider circle of readers. We know nothing of what she has written, since the publication of "*Wild Notes*."

And kisses again that fair young brow,
That meets but a worm's caresses now.

Ye have opened the captive's prison door,
And he stands on his own hearth-stone once more,
And his sire is there with words of blessing,
And his mother with tears and fond caressing,
And a sister's form to his heart is clasped,
And a brother's hand in his own is grasped,
And he feels nor fetter, nor galling chain,—
He is safe! He is free!! He is *home* again!!!

The murderer lies in his murky den,
His crime is hidden from human ken,
Few of his victim's fate may know,
None may tell who hath struck the blow,
But *ye* have brought to his sight again,
Him, whom his own red hand has slain—
With ghastly smile and with glassy eye,
And finger pointing in mockery.
Dreams, ye are strange and fearful things,
When ye come in the might of conscience-stings.

The child lies down in his cradle bed,
His soft hand pillows his drowsy head,
And his parted lips have a cherub smile,
Untouched by sorrow, unstained by guile;
Falls Heaven's light on his baby brow,
And he lists to the "Angel's whisper" now.
Dreams, ye are bright and beautiful things,
When ye visit the child on Seraph's wings.

Not in the hours of sleep alone,
Dreams, is your airy empire won.
Wild tho' the phantoms of midnight are,
Our waking visions are wilder far,
Wilder and vainer; and wise is he
Who taketh them not for reality.

The soldier dreams of the laurel wreath,
As he rushes on to the field of death;
The minstrel dreams of the fadeless bay,
While pouring his soul in his fervid lay;
And the soldier lies with thousands as brave,
And the minstrel filleth a nameless grave.

The statesman dreams of ambition's dower,
Of the pride of wealth, and the pomp of power,
Of a people's trust and a people's love,
That the waning years of his life may prove;
And when age hath palsied both brain and limb,
Oh sad is the waking awaiting him!

The lover dreams of a mortal brow
That shall shine ever blessed and bright as now,
Of an earthly love which no power may change,
No sorrow darken, no time estrange,
That shall know no shadow, no fear, no fall,—
Oh his is the wildest dream of all!

We are dreamers all, we shall still dream on,
Till the vision of life itself be done,
Till the weary race to the goal is run—

Till the fevered pulses are checked and chilled,
Till the fluttering heart is for ever stilled,
Till the final struggle at length is o'er,
And we lie down in quiet to dream no more.

WEAVING.

ISIDORE G. ASCHER.

A maiden was weaving at noonday,
  A maiden with gold-rippling hair,
Whose heart was as warm as the sun-rays
  That softly encircled her there;
And her eyes were like starlights in shadow,
  And her thoughts were like sweet summer air.

I knew by the light of her smiling,
  She was weaving a tissue of dreams,
A web of a million of fancies,
  Illuming her life with their gleams;
That she saw the far future before her
  O'ertinted with halcyon beams.

I did not disturb her with questions,
  Nor mar those sweet thoughts with my own,
For the sunlight that played with her fancies
  From heavenly pathways had flown,
And she wound them in hues of the rainbow,
  As she sat in the noonday alone.

And soon when the shadows had fallen,
  An old man with grey-silvered hair
Was weaving a tissue of visions
  In the gloaming that fell on him there;
And his thoughts were like hues of the evening,
  In the chamber so ghostly and bare.

I knew by the lines on his temples,
  And by the wan smiles on his face,
That from the dead past he was calling
  A host of regrets from their place:
And so he kept weaving his sorrows,
  In a dream that was mournful to trace.

And thus we are weaving forever
  Our hopes, our regrets, and our fears,
And time soon dispels every vision,
  Or we summon them back with our tears;
And still we are none of us wiser,
  As we glide thro' life's current of years!

BIND THE ROSE IN THY GOLDEN HAIR.

W. W. SMITH.

Bind the rose in thy golden hair!—
  Sweetly it blows, and it speaks no sorrow;—
'Tis fanned to-night by the gentle air,
  And washed in the silver dew to-morrow!
Gaily it grows by the green burn-side,
And scatters its sweets o'er the moorland wide,—

Lightly it blooms on the upland lea,
Where the dun-deer trips by the oaken tree,
And scents the gale in the glen below,
Where the maiden lilts to the streamlet's flow;
And wreathes, where the the rose and the hawthorns
gather,
The flowers of Love and Hope together—
Or sings of the time, when in fairy bowers
The rose was crowned the Queen of Flowers.
Queen of flowers the rose shall be,
Bound in the midst of thy locks of yellow!—
Then turn on me thy dark blue e'e,
That is mild as the light of you sunbeam mellow.

Pluck ye the daisy on the lea,—
That gems the green sod with a winsome glory
Fringed with the blushes of morning's e'e,
And silver'd within by the starlight hoary:
Meekly it lifts its humble eye,
And asks but to gaze on the clear blue sky,
And hold up its drop of the pearly dew
To be kissed by the morning winds anew;—
Wherever the rain and the sunbeams fall,
By valley, or hill, or garden wall—
The daisy is scattered, wild and sweet,
And Innocence claims the emblem meet,—
Then bind the daisy on thy breast,
And its leaves unfading there shall rest.
Soft the evening draws her veil,
And the mist on the mountain tops is weeping;
Then gather the rose and the daisy pale,
For my heart in their tender leaves is sleeping.

TOUJOURS FIDÈLE.

ROBERT SWEENY.

Toujours Fidèle, the warrior cried,
As he seized his courser's rein,
And, bending over his weeping bride,
He whispered the hope, which his heart denied,
That they soon might meet again :
And fear not, he said, though the wide, wide sea
Betwixt us its billows swell ;
Believe me, dearest, thy knight will be
To France and to honor—to love and to thee,
Toujours Fidèle.

Then proudly her forehead that lady rears,
And proudly she thus replied—
Nay, think not my sorrow proceeds from fears—
And the glance which she threw, though it shone through
Was the glance of a soldier's bride, [tears,
Not mine is the wish to bid thee stay,
Though I cannot pronounce, "farewell;"
Since glory calls thee—away, away—
And still be thy watch-word on battle day,
Toujours Fidèle.

One moment he gazed—the lingering knight—
The next, to the field he sped :
Why need I tell of the deadly fight,
But to mark his fate ?—for his country's right
He battled—and he bled.

Yet he died as the brave alone can die—
  The conqueror's shout his knell;
His sleep was the slumber of victory—
And for her whom he loved his latest sigh,
    Toujours Fidèle.

THE PASSAGE OF THE BERESINA.*

JOHN BREAKENRIDGE.

Onward! Still on!—the relics of a host
  Whose fame hath made earth's proudest monarchs quake—
They rush, like Ocean's waves, tumultuous, tost—
  Bloodshed and famine mingling in their wake.
There, in one mass, behold the proud array—
The boast of France! Ere yet shall close that day,
  Not e'en *his* voice his minions shall awake;
Nor yet a mother's eye—if such be there—
Shall tell, amid the ghastly heaps, the son she bare!

Onward they press; for ever in their rear
  The foeman sweeps relentless on his way;
The cannon speaks in thunder to the ear;
  No voice can bid that fearful torrent stay;

---

* From "*The Crusades and other Poems*" by JOHN BREAKENRIDGE, published by subscription at Kingston in 1846. This volume possesses considerable poetic merit, though portions of it are somewhat prosaic and diffuse in style. It is distinguished, both in choice of subjects and treatment, by a martial and chivalrous spirit. Three of the poems, "*The Crusades*," "*Napoleon Bonaparte and the French Revolution*," and "*Laiza*," are lengthy poems of an epic character. The volume is probably now out of print.

For flash on flash, and gleaming steel, appear!
What reck they aught of war, save mortal fear,
That bids them not from safety madly stray,
But seek that boon in flight! For, wild and dread,
O'er many a dreary plain the Hettman's Cossacks spread!

Behold the spectral corses grimly strew
Their brethren's path; and all unheeded lie,
Save by the warrior foes' marauding crew,
Whose knives gleam swiftly on the closing eye—
Waked but to hear the curse that bids them die!
And then the banner once that proudly flew,
War-worn and soiled, lies stiff'ning in the hold
Of him who, to his honored standard true,
Binds to his heart that pall with one convulsive fold!

Onward! still on! for now before their view
The sullen river rolls its darkling flood;
The clang of war behind them bursts anew;
No time have they o'er sad defeat to brood.
Onward, o'er dying friends, so late who stood
The sharers of their toil—for life, for life,
The madd'ning race begins! In that dark hour,
With every horror fraught—with danger rife—
Who dreamt of kindred ties, or felt sweet friendship's power?

And fast, and wild, in gathering crowds they come;
And shrieks and groans from out that mingling mass
Tell that the anguished spirit wingeth home
Its weary flight! They win that narrow pass,
But ever and anon the thund'ring bass
Of guns that, rumbling in the distance, boom—
Waking to one continuous peal! Alas!

Is there no hope for that once victor-host?
The despot's arm, earth's scourge, and Gaul's triumphant boast?

None! For the tempest-breath of heaven awakes,
And darkly green the swollen waters flow;
The wintry blast upon them coldly breaks—
The rear-guard yields to the victorious foe!
It heaves—it yawns—O, God! with one dread throe,
The crowded bridge beneath the pressure shakes,
And thrice ten thousand souls are hurled below
Into that "hell of waters," fierce and strong,
Whose waves relentless bear the flower of France along!

Aye! and her vine-clad valleys long shall hear
The voice of mourning for her sons who lie,
Thrown by the sated wave on deserts drear;
And long shall ring "that agonizing cry,"
And haunt his dreams when none to soothe is nigh!
And, fortune flown, shall thunder in his ear
'Mid courts and camps—the worm that ne'er shall die;
And tell to every age, like Heaven's own wrath,
The vengeance dire that waits on the invader's path!

AFTER DEFEAT.

(*From* SAUL.)

CHARLES HEAVYSEGE.

All's over here;—let us withdraw and weep
Down in the red recesses of our hearts,
Or, in our spirits, silent, curse the cravens
Whom uttered execrations too much honor.

Home, home, let us, dishonored,—home if there
Be yet for us a home, and the Philistines
Drive us not forth to miserable exile.
Will they allow us, like to a breathed hare,
Spent, to return and repossess our form ?
Will they endure us in Gibeah ? or must we
Discover some dark den on Lebanon,
And dwell with lions ? or must we with foxes
Burrow, and depend on cunning for our food ?
Better with lions and with foxes mating,
Than be companions of the brood of Israel ;
Yea, better with the hill-wolf famishing,
Than battening with the drove that forms the world.

LITTLE FLORA.

HARRIETT A. WILKINS.

A little bark afloat
On life's rough ocean—
A little flower that blooms
'Mid earth's commotion ;
Long be that fair and time-unwritten brow
As free from lines of mournfulness as now,
And those blue eyes,
Untarnished by the tear, like stars that shine
In summer skies.

We would no blight may pass
Over the blossom ;
We would no storm may rise
O'er ocean's bosom ;

We would—but swelling breakers will be cold,
And sweetest flowers have rootlets in the mould;
 The storm, the clay,
Still mingle with the sunshine and the gold
 Upon our way.

Mother! whose heart of love
 Thy child is blessing—
Father! who with delight,
 Meets her caressing—
O keep the precious flower from dangers free,
And point the voyager to that calm sea
 Where storms come not;
Ah! on the precious treasure given to ye
 Lies Woman's lot.

Her lot, to watch untired
 By beds of anguish;
Her lot, to cheer the heart,
 When Hope's beams languish;
To cheer, and yet to yearn for some kind tone,
That from the board or from the hearth is gone—
 To keep love's lamp
Still burning, beautiful and clear,
 'Mid mist and damp.

Parents! in earnest prayer,
 For this your daughter,
That safe through Life's cold blast,
 And Death's deep water,

A strength o'er which the foe prevaileth not;
A love, that change and time assaileth not—
May win and weep,
Till in the Everlasting Arms,
She falls asleep.

A FRAGMENT.

J. R. RAMSAY.

What phantoms rise and flit along
The silent stream of vanished time:
Forms grief-subdued and still and pale,
As hope transfixed with untold crime.
Even now upon my longing sight
A well remembered scene appears,
Where parted clouds let down the light,
Then close on all the coming years.

Among the sun-fields of the West,
Where roll our country's grandest streams,
There lived a maiden lovelier far
Than fancy's fairest, fondest dreams.
Oft, when the sun's descending beams
Spread splendors o'er the western sky,
We met beneath the blooming thorn
And watched the wondrous glory die.

There, in the golden eventide,
Beneath the fragrant hawthorn tree,
She, whom my spirit deified,
Gave all her promised years to me.

That sun has set. An unknown grave
  Is there alone upon the hill,
And all the scene is silent, save
  The vesper of the whip-poor-will.

Behold! the very hill-side trees
  Seem mourning o'er that lost sun-glow,
And up towards the west their arms
  Wave in the twilight to and fro.
Angels of light who throng the road
  Thro' Hinnom's dim lone solitudes:
My spirit longs for that abode
  Where everlasting stillness broods.

IDEAL LAND.

D. J. WALLACE.

The twilight hour has come again,
  And, like an angel's wing,
It sheds a holy, heavenly calm,
    O'er everything.

Within my soul a quiet reigns.
  And peace and joy flow there,
In noiseless waves, till I have quite
    Forgotten care.

I know not why it is, but yet
  The twilight ever brings
A peace, for which I would not take
    All earthly things.

And while the soul is lulled to rest,
How sweetly do the dreams
Of other days flow back again,
In half-hid streams.

To-day I walked the city's streets,
Where rolls life's varied tide;
And felt alone, though thousands were
Upon each side.

But here, within my little cot,
With Twilight on her throne,
I think of absent ones and feel
I'm *not* alone.

With keys thrown to me by the hand
Of the departed Day,
I ope the portals of a land
Where loved ones stray.

Mysterious land! for there the dead
And living are as one;
O bliss! I meet them all as I
In life have done.

They all seem beings of a clime
Uncursed with grief or care;
And free from toil's corroding hand
They wander there.

Some of them live, and some are dead,
Yet, an unbroken band,
I often meet them all within
Ideal Land.

OUR LITTLE BOY.

E. H. DEWART.

When Autumn had stripped the trees
  Of their gorgeous crimson and gold,
And the murmur of every breeze
  The desolate Winter foretold,
A cherub-boy to our household came—
  Like a beam of golden light
Sent down from the world of joy and love,
  To brighten life's gloomy night.

Our Sunbeam has opened new mines of love,
  Whose wealth was unknown before;
He has kindled a light, in home and heart,
  That shall burn till life is o'er.
We often bend o'er his placid sleep,
  To imprint a kiss on his brow;
Ah! little he knows of the watch we keep,
  And the love that encircles him now—

Every tiny form and childish voice
  Brings our little boy to mind;
He has made my heart to those opening flowers
  More thoughtfully, tenderly, kind.
I hear the patter of little feet
  With emotions before unknown,—
To our joy-lit hearts the world has changed,
  Since baby has taken his throne.

Every playful trick of childish glee
 Has a charm for our wondering eyes;
And even his prattling broken speech
 Seems quaint and wondrously wise.
His eye is bright, and his voice is sweet
 As a wood-bird's matin hymn—
We feel in our silent grateful joy,
 That there never was child like him.

And yet, in the flush of my joy and pride,
 There comes a shadow of pain,
As I wistfully glance along life's tide,
 Towards Eternity's boundless main:
O what if the ruthless Angel of Death,
 Should steal in some fatal hour,
And blight with his terribly icy breath
 Our precious and beautiful flower!

I often muse on his future fate,
 And picture what it may be,
Till darkness comes down on my musing soul,
 Like night on the surging sea.
O which shall he choose, when youth has flown,
 The path of sorrow or joy?
And if I should fall and leave him alone,
 Who will watch o'er my fatherless boy?

Father in heaven! our orisons hear;
 And shield him from sin and from harm;
May our love be tempered with wisdom and fear,
 And our strength be thy holy arm;

May the feet of our darling never stray
  In the paths of folly and woe,
May he choose the pleasures that never decay,
  Above all that sparkle below.

If father and mother should droop and die,
  And sorrowful fortune portend,
Be Thou his defence when danger is nigh,
  A pitying father and friend.
Be Thou his guide through life's perilous way
  Till temptation and conflict are past,
And wherever o'er earth his feet may stray
  Bring him home to Thyself at last.

"OMEMEE"—THE DOVE.

ROBERT S. PATTERSON.

Where the wild-vines creeping,
  Threw a pleasant shade,
Lovely, lone and weeping,
  There stood an Indian maid.
Loudly, sweetly, clearly,
  The piping blue-birds sang—
And through the forest cheerily,
  The voice of insects rang!

She stood there gazing sadly,
  With eyes of midnight hue—
From which the tears gushed madly,
  Like diamond drops of dew;

While the quivering leaves, in pity,
  Were whispering above—
And soothing called her "Omemee!"
"Sweet Omemee!" the dove!

That Indian maid is praying,
  In the forest depths alone:
For her lover's spirit straying—
  To "*Ponemah's** *realm*" has flown—
And now she seeks to follow him,
  Where the "*Baim-wa-wa*" † sounds
To braid his moccasins and belt
  In the happy hunting grounds.

Her mellow tones rose mildly,
  Up through the wafting air;
And the busy echo, wildly,
  Reverberates her prayer
Till rolling o'er the prairies
  To the waters of the west
'Tis heard by "*Gitche Manitou*" ‡
  In the wigwams of the blest.

Gently smiled the Great One
  As he heard Omemee pray,
And pouring forth a cloud storm,
  Upon the blushing day,
It wrapped the trees in dusky folds—
  The teeming earth it kissed—
Then, upward to the sky it rolled,
  Like a noiseless car of mist!

---

*The Land of the Hereafter. † Passing Thunder.
‡ The Great Spirit.

Again through branches peeping,
  The sun shines round and fair—
The wild-vines still are creeping—
  But no Indian maid is there!
For a fountain now is springing
  Where the sweet Omemee stood—
In silvery showers flinging
  Its freshness through the wood!

From that pure spring, flowing;
  A streamlet takes its rise—
Still broad and deeper growing,
  As swift it onward hies:
Fast gurgling o'er the pebbles—
  Smooth, running o'er the sand,
And coying with the rushes,
  Which bend on either hand!

Now through meadows gliding—
  Now tumbling down the hill—
It sweeps through Omemee village,
  And turns the clattering mill,
Through rice swamp, and through forest,
  It wandering winds along;
Till its stream is lost for ever
  In the bosom of "Chemong."

But the trees its flood o'erhanging
  Still breathe Omemee's name,
And the birds through branches flying
  Softly sing the same,

And the "*Mud-wa-aushka*" * sighing
Tells how she died of love;
And men still call Omemee's stream
"The river of the Dove."

GIVEN AND TAKEN.

MRS. J. L. LEPROHON.

The snow-flakes were softly falling
Down on the landscape white,
When the violet eyes of my firstborn
Opened unto the light,
And I thought as I pressed him to me
With loving, rapturous thrill,
He was pure and fair as the snow-flakes
That lay on the landscape still.

I smiled when they spoke of the dreary
Length of the Winter's night,
Of the days so short and gloomy,—
The sun's cold cheerless light—
I listened, but in their murmurs,
Nor word nor thought took part,
For the smiles of my gentle darling
Brought light to my home and heart.

O quickly the joyous spring-time
Came back to our ice-bound earth,
Filling fields and woods with sunshine,
And hearts with hope and mirth;

* The noise of the waves on the shore.

But still on earth's dawning beauty,
  Rested a gloomy shade,
For our tiny household idol
  Began to droop and fade.

Shuddering, I felt that the frailest
  Flower in the old woods dim,
Had perchance a surer and longer
  Lease of life than him:—
In the flush of Summer's beauty,
  On a sunny, golden day,
When flowers gemmed dells and woodlands,
  My blossom passed away.

How I chafed at the brilliant sunshine
  Flooding my lonely room,
How I turned from the sight of nature
  So full of life and bloom,
How I longed for past wintry hours
  With snow-flakes falling fast,
And the little form of my nursling
  In my loving arms clasped.

They put up each tiny garment
  In an attic chamber high,
His coral—his empty cradle—
  That they might not meet my eye;
And his name was never uttered,
  Whate'er each heart might feel,
For they wished that the wound in my bosom
  Might have time to close and heal.

It has done so, thanks to that Power
  That has been my earthly stay,
And should you talk of my darling,
  I could listen now all day.
For I know each passing minute
  Brings me nearer life's last shore,
And nearer that cloudless kingdom
  Where we both shall meet once more.

CONSCIOUS MADNESS.*

(*From* SAUL.)

CHARLES HEAVYSEGE.

What ails me? what impels me on, until
The big drops fall from off my brow? Whence comes
This strange affliction?—Oh, thus to be driven
About!—I will stand still: now move me aught
That can. Ah, shake me, thing; shake me again
Like an old thorn i'th' blast! 'Tis leaving me;
Oh, that it were for ever! Oh, how long
Shall this fierce malady continue, these

* No extract can give any adequate idea of the dramatic power displayed in "SAUL." We have not instituted any comparison between Mr. Heavysege and other distinguished Canadian poets, because the department of poetic art in which he has won high distinction, does not fairly admit of comparison with lyric and descriptive poetry. Mr. Heavysege has received the highest praise from eminent critics, as exhibiting rare subtlety of thought and creative power. But in spite of all this, "SAUL" has shared the neglect and indifference that has hitherto been the birthright of nearly every volume of poetry published in Canada. It is "more in sorrow than in anger," we so frequently refer to this neglect of the productions of Canadian authors, so discreditable to the intelligence, patriotism, and literary taste of the people of Canada.

Dread visitations? See, 'tis here again!
What's here again? Or who? Here's none save I;—
And yet there's some one here. 'Tis here, 'tis here
Within my brain:—no, it is in my heart,—
Within my soul; where rise again black thoughts
And horrible conceptions, that from hell
Might have come up. All blasphemies that my ears
Ever heard; my horridest ideas in dreams;
And impious conceits, that even a fiend
Methinks could scarcely muster, swarm within
Me, rank and black as summer flies on ordure.
Oh, what a den this moment is my breast!
How cold I feel, how cruel and invidious.
Now let no child of mine approach me; neither
Do thou come near to me, Ahinoam,
Their mother and the wife I dearly love;
For now the universe appears one field
On which to spend my rancor. Oh, disperse,
Fit, nor return with thy o'erwhelming shadows!
Oh that it would begone and leave me in
My sorrow! Surely 'tis enough to live
In lone despair. To reign is care enough,
Even in rude health; but to be harassed thus
By an unnamed affliction;—and why harassed?
Oh, why am I thus harassed? I have heard
Of wretches raging under sharp remorse;
Of cruel monarchs, in their latter days,
Falling a prey to an accusing conscience;
But why should I, whose faults smite but myself,
Be thus tormented?

SISERA.

J. READE.

"The mother of Sisera looked out at a window, and cried through the lattice; Why is his chariot so long in coming? why tarry the wheels of his chariot?" &c. —*Judges, v.* 23 *et seq.*

Why comes he not? why comes he not,
  My brave and noble son?
Why comes he not with his warlike men,
  And the trophies his might has won?
How slowly roll his chariot wheels!
  How weary seems the day!
Pride of thy lonely mother's heart,
  Why dost thou still delay?

He comes not yet; will he *never* come,
  To gladden these heavy eyes,
That have watched and watched from morn till eve,
  And again till the sun did rise?
Shall I meet no more his look of joy,
  Nor hear his manly voice?
Why comes he not, with the spoils of war,
  And the damsels of his choice?

Years rolled along in their ruthless course,
  But Sisera came no more,
With his mighty men and his captive maids,
  As he oft had come before.
A *woman's hand* had done the deed
  That laid a hero low;
A *woman's heart* had felt the grief
  That none but mothers know.

TWILIGHT.*

JOHN F. M'DONNELL.

The twilight shrouds the eastern sky,—
  The mist-cloud falls on hill and river,—
The red lights on the water lie,
  And in soft beams of brightness quiver.
The parting day, in one rich cloud
  Of fleecy gold, hangs o'er the city;
And o'er the calm wave echoes loud
  The mariner's wild ringing ditty.
      With murmurs deep,
      Like troubled sleep,
  The mighty tide is onward flowing;—
      And, see, afar,
      The Evening Star;—
  Its lonely ray, in beauty, glowing.

The northern sky looks dim and grey,—
  The mountain tops are clothed in shadow,—
The night breeze wanders forth, in play;
  And, rippling, breathes across the meadow;
The scented buds their leaflets close;
  The dew-drops gleam on tree and flower;—
And Nature, with new beauty, glows
  Beneath the witching twilight hour:

* It is to be regretted, that one who can write so musically, and with such deep appreciation of nature's beauty and power, should renounce the muses, to the extent Mr. McDonnell has latterly done. Mr. McDonnell formerly contributed extensively, both to the American and Canadian press, but has, we believe, written scarcely any poetry for several years past. He is a native of Quebec, born in 1838, a member of the legal profession, and at present connected with the Quebec press.

While, o'er my soul,
Bright fancies roll,
That drive away the gloom of sorrow,
And bid me still,
In good or ill,
Hope for a better, happier morrow.

I love to see the noon of day,
In sunny robes of splendor beaming;
I love to see the wavelets play,
Beneath the silvery moonlight streaming:—
But sweeter far than sun or moon,—
The glories of the purple even,
When Night's dark mantle spreads, too soon,
Across the bright expanse of heaven.
Thus Beauty's bloom
Ends in the tomb;
By breath of Time, its glories shaded;—
Thus Pleasure's flower
Blooms for an hour;
Then—like the twilight eve—'tis faded.

WEARY.

J. H. KING.

Build me a cot by some woodland stream,
Some lonely spot where my heart may dream,
Where nought of song save the streamlet's flow
May call me back to the long ago:
And make me a couch of the lichen green,
That wraps the grove with its emerald sheen:

Oh, build me a cot in the dark green wood,
Where the hum of life may never intrude!

I pine for the place where the wild bird's throat
Yields the only song my ear can note;
Or the silver hymn of the mountain rill
As it leaps from its home in the rock-bound hill.
I long for the place where the matin song
Is lost in the solemn vespers' throng,
By a vast unbroken silence awed
That speaks of an ever-present God.

I weary to flee from this constant strife,
This ceaseless clangor, this clash of life;
I long for a place by no power possessed,
Where my heart can whisper, here is rest.
I have sought for this place in the lordly hall,
In the peasant's cot where life's shadows fall,
'Mid the sorrowing group, mid the joyous fair,
I've searched them all, but it was not there.

Oh where shall I seek,—without,—within,—
That earth hath no leprosy of sin;
That the power of ambition, the pride of wealth,
Hath not stained the heart or poisoned health?
Aye, where shall I seek for solitude,
Free from the taint of earth's harpy brood?
E'en solitude, could I find her cell,
Would shrink away from her own voice knell.

The past, where cherished memories rife
Are sadly counting the sands of life;
The past is there, but her wreath of flowers
Is withered and dead; they fall in showers

O'er the urn of hope, where cold and lone,
Her relics repose without a stone;
No wreath, no relic Falernian-crowned,
Save one lonely spot, a grassy mound.

And I, oh, alas! where shall I flee
To find that rest that's so dear to me,
I've sought it in vain and wearied now,
I turn from the search with an aching brow.
But I must seek in a brighter clime
Afar beyond the shadows of time;
I'll seek it there—earthly gain is loss—
And rest in the shade of the hallowed cross.

THE SHIPWRECK.*

SAMUEL PAYNE FORD.

Gallantly over the proud sea's foam
  Doth the noble vessel ride,
She hath braved the storm in her voyage home,
  And the hurricane's blast defied;
Full faithfully hath she borne her load
  To the far-off sunny shore,
And over the Storm-King's dark abode
  Is returning home once more.

Hopefully to their rest at night
  Go an anxious-hearted band,
For the captain hath said, "With the morning light
  You shall gaze on the wished-for land."

---

* Mr. FORD was born and brought up in the neighbourhood of Peterborough. His poetry is distinguished by purity and elevation of moral sentiment, strong, human sympathies, and sweetness and gracefulness of style.

And with many a dream of home and friends,
  And of loved ones far away,
Drawn near by the charm that dreamland lends,
  They wait for the coming day.

But, alas! ere the water-weed shall bow
  To the morning's perfumed breath,
There are many who dream so peacefully now
  Shall sleep the sleep of Death;
For the dark-winged angel is hovering nigh,
  And brooding above the deck,
And the morn shall reveal to the passer-by
  Not even a shapeless wreck.

The mysterious midnight hour is past,
  With naught to affright or harm,
When wild and high on the wailing blast
  There is borne a fierce alarm;
And the dreamers awake from their peaceful sleep,
  Aroused by the sudden shock,
To find, alas! that their noble ship
  Hath struck on a sunken rock.

There were many and mingled cries that night,
  Arose on the stormy air;
Loud anxious calls for the morning light,
  And a few low sounds of prayer;
We know not but their prayers were heard
  By the God who rules the wave,
But at morn the winds and the wild sea-bird
  Sang a requiem over their grave.

ROSA.

JOHN READE.

Thou art gone, sweet love, to take thy rest,
Like a weary child, on thy mother's breast;
And thou hearest not, in thy calm deep sleep,
The voices of those that around thee weep.

Thou art gone, where the weary find a home,
Where sickness and sorrow can never come:
A flower too fair for earthly skies
Thou art gone to bloom in Paradise.

Thou art gone, and I hear not thy gladsome tone,
But my heart is still beating "*alone, alone*,"—
Yet often in dreams do I hear a strain
As of angels bearing thee back again.

Thou art gone, and the *world* may not miss thee long,
For thou didst not care for its idle throng;
But this fond bosom, in silent woe,
Shall carry thine image wherever I go.

Thou art gone, thou art gone; shall we meet no more
By the sandy hill or the winding shore?
Or watch as the crested billows rise,
And the frightened curlew startling cries?

Thou art gone, but oh! in that land of peace
Where sin, and sorrow and anguish cease,
Where all is happy and bright and fair,
My own sweet love, may I meet thee *there!*

LAY HER DOWN SILENTLY.

REV. H. F. DARNELL, M. A.

Lay her down *silently*
'Neath the green grass;
Like dews of the morning,
Her spirit doth pass;
Why shouldst thou mourn her
With sob or with sigh?
Angels have shrined her
In glory on high.

Lay her down *hopefully;*
Earth's flowers die
Ere the keen blasts of winter
Go bitterly by;
But she, like those flowers,
Shall blossom anew,
When the Spring of Eternity
Breaks on the view.

Lay her down *trustingly;*
Dear though she be,
Is she not dearer
To Christ than to thee?
Though now from thy treasure
His wisdom may sever,
'Tis only to give her thee
Brighter than ever.

Lay her down *fearlessly ;*
Darkness and doom
May fold their deep wings
Over her, and her tomb ;
But the dawn of Eternity
Scatters each cloud,
Gives garments of glory
For pall and for shroud.

Lay her down *thankfully ;*
Let her sleep on;
Learn to say cheerfully
" God's will be done !"
The scenes of futurity
Thou canst not know,
May be He takes her
From guilt or from woe.

Lay her down *prayerfully*—
Not that she needs
Now the deep words
With which man intercedes;
But pray that her exodus,
Sad though it be,
May open a pathway
To glory for thee.

THE LIGHT IN THE WINDOW PANE.

CHARLES SANGSTER.

A joy from my soul's departed,
A bliss from my heart is flown,
As weary, weary-hearted,
I wander alone—alone!

The night wind sadly sigheth
  A withering, wild refrain,
And my heart within me dieth
  For the light in the window pane.

The stars overhead are shining,
  As brightly as e'er they shone,
As heartless—sad—repining,
  I wander alone—alone!
A sudden flash comes streaming,
  And flickers adown the lane,
But no more for me is gleaming
  The light in the window pane.

The voices that pass are cheerful,
  Men laugh as the night winds moan;
They cannot tell how fearful
  'Tis to wander alone—alone!
For them, with each night's returning,
  Life singeth its tenderest strain,
Where the beacon of love is burning—
  The light in the window pane.

Oh sorrow beyond all sorrows
  To which human life is prone:
Without thee, through all the morrows,
  To wander alone—alone!
Oh dark, deserted dwelling!
  Where Hope like a lamb was slain,
No voice from thy lone walls welling,
  No light in thy window pane.

But Memory, sainted angel!
  Rolls back the sepulchral stone,
And sings like a sweet evangel:
  "No—never, never alone!
True grief has its royal palace,
  Each loss is a greater gain;
And Sorrow ne'er filled a chalice
  That Joy did not wait to drain!"

INVOCATION.

W. H. HAWLEY.

Spirits of earth! Spirits of air!
  Come to me over the silver sea;
Lay the locks of my tangled hair,
  For the lov'd, the lost one is coming to me!

I see her sailing on yon light cloud,
  With wreaths of roses upon her hung,
And wildly around her moon-beam shroud
  Her glistening locks of jet are flung.

I see the light of her polished brow—
  I feel the beam of her laughing eye!
Come, invisible Spirits, now,
  And bear me away to yonder sky!

Spirits of earth! Spirits of air!
  Throw your spells on the flying shade!
For she slowly fades from the moon-light's glare,
  And tells me not where her rest is made.

GLIMPSES OF HIGHLAND SUPERSTITION.

DONALD M'INTOSH.

O Superstition! though beset
By Erudition's gun and net,
And made ignobly to retreat
Before the pedant's rod;
Yet do thy visions dread seem fair
To me who breath'd the mountain air,
And sought the red-deer's secret lair
'Mid wilds but seldom trod;—

Wilds haunted by the lone Banshee
Whom shepherds in the gloaming see,
As homeward hums the laden bee,
And midges skim the lake;
When all beside in silence sleeps,
Save cascades rushing down the steeps,
And Echo, whom their music keeps
Perpetually awake.

Then forth thou led'st thy spirit-host—
Of goblin, kelpie, witch and ghost
Of wanderer in the snowdrift lost,
When madly raved the storm—
Lost where now oft with smothered wail
And hollow eye, and visage pale,
And noiseless step, along the vale
Is seen that shadowy form!

And quaintly dressed in robes of green
Elfins may then be dimly seen,
Attendant on their sylvan Queen
Upon some mossy knoll;
Or with flint-pointed arrows keen
Waylaying mortals who in vain
May there be seeking to regain
The child the fairies stole!

The scene is changed—and, hark that sound!
Yon rocky cave a tongue hath found,
And hunter's voice and bay of hound
Are on the night-wind borne;
And shades of Fingal and his band,
Who once inhabited the land,
Soon issue forth with bow in hand
And far-resounding horn.

The chase awakes the sleeping Night,
The phantom stag bounds far in flight,
The traveller, shuddering with affright,
Prays Heaven his path to guide;
The fox seeks out his den secure,
The house-dog crouches on the floor,
While fast along the heathy moor
Those spectral hunters glide!

Such, Superstition, is thy might—
Thus dost thou people Scotia's night;
Oft have I faced with dread delight
Its glamour and its gloom.

'Tis true we have no warlocks here,
No haunted dells, no sprites to fear,
Yet do I not the less revere
    My own loved Highland home.

Dread Power! full well I mind the day,
When thought of vengeful ghost or fay
Sufficed my wayward steps to stay
    From evil deed or word.
Let sceptics, if they will, ignore—
Better that such as own thy power
Believe the truth AND SOMETHING MORE,
    THAN BOTH ALIKE DISCARD.

THE GREY LINNET.*

JAMES M'CARROLL.

There's a little grey friar in yonder green bush,
Clothed in sackcloth—a little grey friar
Like a druid of old in his temple—but, hush
He's at vespers: you must not go nigher.

Yet, the rogue! can those strains be addressed to the skies,
And around us so wantonly float,
Till the glowing refrain like a shining thread flies
From the silvery reel of his throat?

When he roves, though he stains not his path through the air
With the splendor of tropical wings,
All the lustre denied to his russet plumes there,
Flashes forth through his lay when he sings.

---

* There is exquisite humour, and true poetry, in this little piece. Mr. McCarroll has been long and favourably known to the Canadian public as a writer of verse. He is a native of Ireland; and at present resides in Toronto.

For the little grey friar's so wondrous wise,
Though in such a plain garb he appears,
That on finding he can't reach your soul through your eyes,
He steals in through the gates of your ears.

But, the cheat!—'tis not heaven he's warbling about—
Other passions, less holy, betide—
For, behold! there's a little grey nun peeping out
From a bunch of green leaves at his side.

WORDS.

JOHN READE.

Every heart that throbs must know
  Fountains sweet and bitter;
Either we may cause to flow,
  By the words we utter.

Idle words may pierce the deep
  Of the gentlest spirit,—
Waking sorrow from its sleep,
  Treading roughly near it.

Words of love may lull to rest
  Care, or grief, or anguish,—
Rousing hope within the breast,
  Where it seemed to languish.

Then let none misuse the gift
  God for use has given;
Through him, every word may lift
  Some one nearer heaven.

WHY DO YOU ENVY ME?

WILLIAM WYE SMITH.

I have an estate in the Land of Dreams,
And thither I often flee,
It brings me joy in as many streams
As any wealth I see;—
And you may lay claim to a wide domain
That lies by a sunny sea;
Then go to the land where I have been,
For why do you envy me?

I have a sweet bark on the sea of love,
That carries me whither I will,—
With its gleaming wings like an arrowy dove,
And the sun on its pathway still;—
There's gems at hand on the farther strand,
And pearls beneath our lee—
There's other barks on the golden sand,
Then why do you envy me?

I have a light heart in this breast of mine,
Like a singing bird in June,
Or a sparkling stream where the roses twine,
That murmurs its endless tune.
I look for my share of toil and care,
Nor yet shall unhappy be;—
A conscience at rest will make you blest,
Then why do you envy me?

TO MY SON.*

WILLIAM WYE SMITH.

Too gentle for the ruder winds of earth
To chill and wither—
Too many tokens of a heavenly birth
Not to flee thither—
No wish of mine, though it had magic worth,
Should draw thee hither.

For I am sad amid these damps sublunar,
But happy thou!
And I shall doubtless wear that Peace the sooner
Upon my brow—
That I am left, like vine behind the pruner,
Lopp'd in each bough!

Yet oh my heart goes out in bitter yearning,
For love so lost!—
A smouldering fire whose embers still are burning
On altar toss'd,
That human pride, that only now is learning
How love is cross'd.

---

* "ALAZON AND OTHER POEMS" was published by Mr. Smith, at Toronto, in 1850. Though some of the pieces are not free from signs of immaturity, yet, as a whole, the volume contained much promise. "ALAZON," the longest poem, though rather too fanciful and unreal in its general conception, evinced a mastery of the difficulties of the Spenserian stanza, that was in itself an omen of higher achievements. The pieces by Mr. Smith in this volume, with the exception of "BIND THE ROSE," have been written since the publication of "ALAZON." Mr. Smith is a native of Jedburgh, Scotland, born in 1827. He has resided in Canada for many years; and is at present editor of the *Owen Sound Times* and of the *Sunday-School Dial.*

O Loved and Lost! 'tis thus the lot of all:—
The loved are gone—
And lost to circle of the hearth and hall
The Angel One
That come to every house—whom Angels call
Too soon upon!

MINNIEBEL.

PAMELIA S. VINING.

Where the willow weepeth
By a fountain lone,
Where the ivy creepeth,
O'er a mossy stone,
With pale flowers above her,
In a quiet dell,
Far from those who love her,
Slumbers Minniebel.

There thy bed I made thee,
By that fountain side,
And in anguish laid thee
Down to rest, my bride!
Tenderest and fairest,
Who thy worth may tell?
Flower of beauty rarest,
Saintly Minniebel!

Weary years have borrowed
From my eye its light,

Time my cheek has furrowed,
And these locks are white;
But my heart will ever
'Mid its memories dwell,
Fondly thine forever,
Angel Minniebel.

IMPROMPTU ON A BEAUTIFUL BUTTERFLY.

JAMES M'CARROLL.

Frailest of all earth's lovely things,
Uncertain wanderer that swings
Upon those gaudy, rose-leaf wings
In yonder sky,
What of the blight that Autumn brings
To thee by and by?

Half helpless in the summer air,
The sport of wanton breezes there,
How, thoughtless creature, shalt thou bear
The ruthless blast
That, with the chill of time and care,
Strikes thee at last?

Flushed gossamer, thou hast thy day—
Thy morn and noon of sunny play;
And, sportive creature, tell me, pray,
What more have we?
We flutter, too, and pass away,
Bright thing, like thee.

DAWN.

JAMES M'CARROLL.

With folded wings of dusky light
  Upon the purple hills she stands,
An angel between day and night,
  With tinted shadows in her hands—

Till suddenly transfigured there,
  With all her dazzling plumes unfurl'd,
She climbs the crimson flooded air
  And flies in glory o'er the world!

TAAPOOKAA—A HURON LEGEND.

CHARLES SANGSTER.

The clouds roll over the pine trees,
  Like waves that are charged with ire;
Golden and glory-hued their crests,
  Ablaze with a gorgeous fire.

The sun has gone down in splendor,
  The heavens are wild with flame,
And all the horizon is burning
  With colors that have no name.

And over the mighty forests
  The mystical hues are spread,
As calm as the smiles of angels,
  As still as the peaceful dead.

And the lake, serene and thoughtful,
And the river, deep in dreams,
And the purple cliff in the distance,
Are robed with the glory-gleams,

Until earth seems a sacred temple,
Where spirits of light have trod,
Where man should not dare to enter;
Too sacred for aught but God.

Calm eve over lovely Huron,
Calm eve in the sombre wild,
And over the rude bark wigwam
Of the swarthy forest-child.

There's a gathering of the red men,
Of their youths and maidens fair,
Of the mothers of braves and heroes,
And the feast is spreading there.

From the banks of the Cadaracqui,
From Niagara's solitudes,
Where the song of the Water Spirit
Rolled vast through the primal woods:

From Superior's rocky défiles,
Her grand and rugged shores,
From Utawa and blue-waved Erie,
Came the Chiefs and Sagamores,

Bringing gifts from the distant lodges,
Rare gifts for the lovely bride—
Taapookaa, the fairest maiden
That ever for true-love sighed.

Taapookaa, the loved, the lovely,
  No beauty was there like hers,
And through all the tribes of the forest
  The Braves were her worshippers.

But where is her young Sioux lover,
  The pride of her trusting heart?
The Brave that her love hath chosen,
  Whose life is of hers a part.

Away from the bridal revels,
  Away from the feast, he roves,
Alone over lonely rivers,
  Alone in the lonely groves!

Taapookaa must wed another,
  The Chief of a neighboring tribe;
Neither force nor friends can save her,
  Neither tear nor prayer can bribe!

For this have the Chieftains gathered,
  Great Chiefs from the wilds afar;
They have prayed to Manitou freely,
  And saluted the Bridal Star.

All things for the feast are ready,
  All ripe for the revelry,
And the bridegroom-chief is waiting,—
  But Taapookaa, where is she?

Like the zephyr that bends the flowers,
  That bendeth but may not break,
So, lightly, her footstep treadeth
  The cliff o'er the calmy lake.

The stars are all weeping for her,
  The moon hath a look forlorn,
For the beautiful maid, all blushes,
  All blushes, and truth, and scorn!

The breeze has a mournful cadence,
  A sigh for the fairest fair;
It cooleth her maiden blushes,
  And fingers her jetty hair.

Like a tragic queen she standeth,
  On the jagged cliff alone;
All nature has paused to shudder,
  And the stricken forests moan.

A prayer for her young Sioux lover,
  That wanders the wilds forlorn,
And she leaps from the cliff, all daring,
  And maidenly truth, and scorn.

At night when the stars are shining,
  And the moon, with silvery hue,
Illumines the lake with radiance,
  Is seen a white canoe:

Two shadowy forms within it,
  Two faces that seem to smile,—
The maid and her brave Sioux lover
  Returned from the Spirit-Isle.

GARIBALDI!

ALEX. M'LACHLAN.

O sons of Italy awake,
Your hearths and altars are at stake,—
Arise, arise, for Freedom's sake,
And strike with Garibaldi !

The Liberator now appears,
Foretold by prophets, bards and seers,
The hero sprung from blood and tears,
All hail to Garibaldi!

Let serfs and cowards fear and quake,—
O Venice, Naples, Rome awake,
Like lava of your burning lake,
Rush on with Garibaldi!

Up and avenge your country's shame,
Like Ætna belching forth her flame,
Rush on in freedom's holy name,
And strike with Garibaldi!

'Tis freedom thunders in your ears;
The weary night of blood and tears,
The sorrows of a thousand years,
Cry, On with Garibaldi!

The shades that hover round your fanes,
The blood of heroes in your veins,
Keep shouting, Rise and break your chains,
And on with Garibaldi!

And tongues in many a dungeon stone,
And prison walls are shouting on,
And sweep the madman from his throne,
Then on with Garibaldi!

The Roman Eagle is not dead,
Her mighty wings again are spread,
To swoop upon the tyrant's head,
And strike with Garibaldi!

The drum of Bomba's doom does beat,
The shadows of the murdered meet,
To drag him to the judgment seat,
Then on with Garibaldi!

The land wherein the laurel waves,
Was never meant to nourish slaves,
Then onward to your bloody graves,
Or live like Garibaldi!

DRINK.

I. G. ASCHER.

There's a sound of woe in the cheerless street,
And a shriek in the midnight air,
For a drunken sot is reeling along,
In the gathering darkness there;
And I hear the meaningless words that come
From the depths of his heart's despair;
'Tis a moan for drink,—
For he'll drink and drink,

Till the earth seems to reel and swim—
  Till his hope in God and his trust in man
Are lost in his pitiless cries—
  Till he loathes his life, and so loathing, dies,
      And all for the sake of drink!

He cries not for aid from a merciful God,
  He craves not a pittance of bread,
But shrieks for drink to the hollow winds,
  That echo his tottering tread;
And his fleshless bones clasp the cold, dumb stones,
  That serves for his pillow and bed,—
      For he'll drink and drink
      Till his eyes are dim—
  Till his senses ache with pain,—
For his trust in God and his faith in man
  He'll never on earth regain.
While he hates the sight of both day and night
  For the sake of the demon drink!

Has he sipped the cup of a direful doom?
  Has care made him grovel low?
Has penury cankered his youthful hopes,
  Or darkened their rainbow glow?
Has Heaven deserted this homeless man
  Whose words seem the gasping of woe?
      'Tis the poison drink
      That maddens the brain—
  That has made his bosom a hell,
While a drunkard's gloom, like a fearful doom
  In his heart and home does dwell,
Where fell disease and famine have sped,—
  And all for the sake of drink!

Raise him from where he crouches and creeps
  On the slime and mud at his feet,—
Bear him where blessings shall scatter in night,
  The curses his lips would repeat;
Raise him, but banish the maddening cup—
  The curse of the home and street,—
And wage a war with the demon drink,
  The tempter to crime below,
That makes a hell of the purest dell,
  Where flowers might bloom and grow—
That surely gives birth on this beautiful earth
  To the direst sin and woe.

THE PRODIGAL'S SOLILOQUY.

SAMUEL PAYNE FORD.

Ah! I know it; the way of transgressors is hard;
I have walked in that way, and I have my reward;
I have drained off the fluid that flashed in the bowl,
And the poison it held is destroying my soul.

I have revelled for years 'mid the pleasures of earth,
Have been drunk with its music, its madness, its mirth,
But the fruits, fair as dew which the honey-bee sips,
Like the apples of Sodom, were dust on my lips.

I have sown my wild oats with a bountiful hand,
And cherished their growth with the fat of the land,
But alas! in the premature blight of my years,
I am reaping the harvest of trouble and tears.

Long ago, when the flowers of my youth were in bloom,
And the song-birds enlivened the dear halls of home,
I seemed happy, almost as the angels above,
While I bathed in the sunlight of friendship and love.

But the flowers are all faded, the songsters have flown,
And both homeless and hopeless, I wander alone,
Not a dear one to love me, nor friend to console,
Though I lavished on *friends* all the wealth of my soul.

The fair, fragile form of my mother is laid
Where the cypress and willow wave over her head,
And the true, noble heart upon which she relied,
Lies ruthlessly broken and torn by her side.

They had prayed for their boy with unfaltering faith,
Till their footsteps went down in the river of Death,
And their last exclamation, ere set of the sun,
Was, "O, Father, remember the wandering one."

And that sisterly voice that implored me to stay,
When I spoke of my purpose to wander away,
Is rejoicing, perchance, in yon bright world of bliss,
For I heard it no more 'mid the shadows of this.

Oh! a flood of fierce anguish continues to roll,
Like a tempest of fire, o'er my agonized soul,
For I know, by a torturing instinct I have,
That I hurried them on to a premature grave.

I would pray, but a mountain of guilt rises up,
Shutting out from my soul the last vestige of hope;
And like Cain I am forced in my utter despair,
To exclaim, "It is more than my spirit can bear!"

And while others are gaining the portals of bliss,
I am nearing a torture more dreadful than this,
Where the worm dieth not, and the flames of the fire,
Like a burning volcano, flash brighter and higher.

But stay! what is that? 'tis a sound that I hear,
Falling, soft as the dropping of dew on my ear;
It resembles a voice that I heard long ago,
Ere my soul had grown wayward, and callous with woe.

And it bids me look up, nor by doubt be deterred,
For the prayers that were offered for me have been heard,
And the Angel of Mercy is now on the road,
To convey the repenting one back to his God.

Ah, mother! thy pleadings are answered at last,
Though the day of salvation seemed certainly past:
And I cherish a hope that when life shall be o'er,
Thou wilt welcome me home to the glorified shore.

CHILDHOOD.

J. J. PROCTER.

Blushes are on the snow
    Where the Western sun is dying,
And night comes creeping above and below,
    And the evening breeze is sighing;
I sit by my little one's bed
    Watching her quiet sleep,
While around on the fire-lit wall and o'erhead
    The flickering shadows creep;

Watching the blaze that streams
    From the ruddy lips of the fire,
And my child that sleeps while its mother dreams
    Of her darling babe and its sire—
What in the days to come,
    Shall my own little one be?
The pride and the joy of her happy home,
    And her God's to eternity?

How sweetly the downcast lid
    On the sleeping eye reposes,
And the bloom of her cheek, half seen, half hid,
    Gleams like the buds of roses.
The little hand is at rest,
    Under the golden hair,
And the snow-white coverlet over her breast
    Seems scarce with her breath to stir.

What does my baby see,
    That a smile comes over her face?
Does my pretty one think of her father and me,
    And her little sister's grace?
What childish fancy pleases her now
    That she looks so sweet and mild,
And brightens up from lip to brow,
    With the grave calm smile of a child?

A smile, and nothing more,
    Quiet and soft, and seldom seen,
Stealing like summer breezes o'er,
    And leaving the baby face serene;

A ripple upon the wave,
    Fading away in the joy of its birth,
And leaving the water calm and grave,
    In a beauty not known by earth.

Is she not mine, God-given?
    And now, when she laughs in her dreams, I know
Her angel speaks with her Father in heaven,
    Of her who sees Him in visions below:
I gaze with awe, and with half-stayed breath,
    For methinks, not faintly shadowed, I trace
The peace that I pray may be hers till death,
    And the joy that rests on an angel's face.

THE LITTLE SHOES.

CHARLES SANGSTER.

Her little shoes! we sit and muse
    Upon the dainty feet that wore them;
By day and night our souls' delight
    Is just to dream and ponder o'er them.
We hear them patter on the floor;
    In either hand a toy or rattle;
And what speaks to our hearts the more—
    Her first sweet words of infant prattle.

I see the face so fair, and trace
    The dark-blue eye that flashed so clearly;
The rose-bud lips, the finger-tips
    She learned to kiss—O, far too dearly!

The pearly hands turned up to mine,
  The tiny arms my neck caressing;
Her smile, that made our life divine,
  Her silvery laugh—her kiss, a blessing.

Her winning ways, that made the days
  Elysian in their grace so tender,
Through which Love's child our souls beguiled
  For seeming ages starred with splendor:
No wonder that the angel-heirs
  Did win our darling life's-joy from us,
For she was theirs—not all our prayers
  Could keep her from the Land of Promise.

THE CHILD OF PROMISE.

A TRANSLATION FROM THE GAELIC OF EVAN M'COLL, BY THE LATE REV. DR. BUCHANAN, OF METHVEN, PERTHSHIRE.

She died—as die the roses
  On the ruddy clouds of dawn,
When the envious sun discloses
  His flame, and morning's gone.

She died—like waves of sun-glow
  Fast by the shadows chased;
She died—like heaven's rainbow
  By gushing showers effaced.

She died—like flakes appearing
  On the shore beside the sea;
Thy snow as bright! but, nearing
  The ground-swell broke on thee.

She died—as dies the glory
  Of music's sweetest swell;
She died—as dies the story
  When the best is still to tell.

She died—as dies moon beaming
  When scowls the rayless wave;
She died—like sweetest dreaming,
  That hastens to its grave.

She died—and died she early:
  Heaven wearied for its own.
As the dipping sun, my Mary,
  Thy morning ray went down!

THE SONG OF A GLORIFIED SPIRIT.

GEORGE MARTIN.

A youth knelt down by a new made grave,
  Unseen by the world, and wept;
A sister whose beauty no love could save
  Beneath in the darkness slept.

'Twas a calm sweet eve, and on hill and plain
  The summer had lavished her dower;
But the full, full heart of the youth could gain
  No solace from sun or flower.

The big warm tears he wiped from his cheek,
  As he thought, with a struggling faith,
"O God, if I could but hear her speak!—
  O mystical Life of Death!"

In silence and sorrow he lingered long,
And just as he rose to depart,
In the heavens was warbled this saintly song,
Which fell like a balm on his heart:

"Beautiful are my walks in the sky,
Beautiful, beautiful!
Here the amaranths never die,
Here the sweet winds murmur and sigh—
Beautiful, beautiful!

"Joyfully glide my golden hours,
Joyfully, joyfully!
Here the leaves of the hyacinth flowers
Whisper around my love-lit bowers—
Joyfully, joyfully!

"Lovingly smile my comrades here,
Lovingly, lovingly!
All the bright shapes of this blissful sphere
Tell how that each unto each is dear—
Lovingly, lovingly!

"Merciful is my Father, my all,
Merciful, merciful!
Here the white-cheeked lilies, so tall,
Sing in their place by the jasper wall—
Merciful, merciful!"

A NORTHERN RUNE.

CHARLES SANGSTER.

Loud rolleth the rune, the martial rune
Of the Norse-King-Harpist bold;
He's proud of his line, he's erect as the pine
That springs on the mountains old.
Through the hardy North, when his song goes forth,
It rings like the clash of steel;
Yet we have not a fear, for his heart's sincere,
And his blasts we love to feel.

Chorus :

Then, hi! for the storm,
The wintry storm,
That maketh the stars grow dim:
Not a nerve shall fail,
Not a heart shall quail,
When he rolls his grand old hymn.

O, hale and gay is that Norse-king gray,
And his limbs are both stout and strong;
His eye is as keen as a falchion's sheen
When it sweeps to avenge a wrong.
The Aurora's dance is his merry glance,
As it speeds through the starry fields;
And his anger falls upon Odin's Halls
Like the crash of a thousand shields.
Then, hi! for the storm, &c.

His stately front has endured the brunt
Of Scythian rack and gale,
As the vengeful years clashed their icy spears
On the boss of his glancing mail;
When he steps in his pride from his Halls so wide
He laughs with a wild refrain,
And the Elfins start from the iceberg's heart,
And echo his laugh again.
Then, hi! for the storm, &c.

When the woods are stirred by the antlered herd,
He comes like a Nimrod bold,
And the forest groans as his mighty tones
Swoop down on the startled fold;
In his mantle white he defies the Night,
With the air of a King so free:
Then hurra for the rune, the North-King's rune,
For his sons, his sons are we.
Then, hi! for the storm, &c.

SUMMER-EVENING.

AUGUSTA BALDWYN.

Calm is the evening. Not a ripple stirs
The crystal waters of yon limpid stream,
That blushes deep beneath the last bright ray
The sun has left at parting, and which throws
A lovely radiance round. Not e'en the breeze
Ruffles a moment one pure tranquil wave,
But breathes soft whisp'ring music through the woods,
Bending the flowers on the mossy shores,

And graceful willows o'er the silent brooks,
To bathe in coolness there. Afar the hills
Are glowing in the sunshine; while below
O'er the low valley gentle evening casts
Her veil of pensive shades. I love this hour
Of melancholy calmness, for my heart.
Hath sympathy from nature. O I feel
No more my spirit's loneliness; no more
I sigh for draughts to fill the longing mind,
The bosom's emptiness. My spirit soars,
And seems to roam 'mid nature's loveliness,
And in her beauties and her stillness finds
Mysterious happiness. The gentle air,
Laden with odor from the sylvan groves,
Breathes bliss around me, and its low sweet voice
Seems the soft whisperings of joy to soothe
The weary heart; and softly peace descends,
Lulls to repose the ruffled waves of grief,
Casts to oblivion every earthly thought,
Making fair Nature's solitudes appear
Fraught with some bliss of heaven, for we feel
The presence of Jehovah! His power is seen,
His works proclaim him, and his voice is heard
In nature's harmonies.

CALL ME BY MY CHRISTIAN NAME.

WILLIAM P. LETT.

Call me by my Christian name,
'Tis sweetest to my ear:
Far dearer than the voice of fame,
From Friendship's lips to hear

The fond familiar accents of Youth's dear days gone by,
When life was young, and Hope's fair star shone brilliantly on high.

Call me by my Christian name,
If thou art of the few
Who with me in the garden
Of happy childhood grew:
If thou art one with whom I played when life was in its spring,
Thou art welcome thus to call me as the Robin is to sing.

Together to the village school
We went for many a day;
Together on the self-same stool
Perhaps we've whiled away
The hours, when "the master's" eye was wandering elsewhere;
Then call me by my Christian name just as you did when there.

The wanderer returning home
From some far-distant strand,
Treads anxiously the pathways
Of his own loved native land:
He sees but strangers, till a voice falls sweetly on his ear;
He hears his name, he's home again, some friend of youth is near.

Then call me by my Christian name:
Whatever be my lot,
I would not that the cherished sound
Should ever be forgot;
In memory's magic numbers it strikes the sweetest key;
Then call me by my Christian name, 'tis music still to me.

O THE DAYS WHEN I WAS YOUNG!

J. W. D. MOODIE.

O the days when I was young!
  A playful little boy,
When my piping treble rung
  With the notes of early joy.
O the sunny days of Spring!
  When I sat beside the shore
And heard the wild-birds sing:
  Shall I never hear them more?

And the daisies scattered round,
  Half hid amid the grass,
Lay like gems upon the ground
  Too gay for me to pass.
How sweet the milk-maid sung,
  As she sat beside her cow,
How clear her wild notes rung;
  There's no music like it now.

As I watched the ship's white sail,
  'Mid the sunbeams on the sea,
Spreading canvas to the gale,
  How I longed with her to be;
I thought not of the storm
  And the wild cries on her deck,
When writhed her graceful form
  'Mid the hurricane and wreck.

And I launched my little ship
  With her sails, and hold beneath,
Deep laden on each trip,
  With berries from the heath.
Ah! little did I know,
  When I longed to be a man,
Of the gloomy cares and woe
  That meet in life's brief span.

O the happy nights I lay
  With my brothers in our beds!
Where we soundly slept, till day
  Shone brightly o'er our heads;
And the blessed dreams that came
  To fill my heart with joy,—
O that I now could dream
  As I dreamt—a little boy!

The sun shone brighter then,
  And the moon more soft and clear,
For the wiles of crafty men
  I had not learned to fear;
But all seemed fair and gay,
  With the fleecy clouds above,
I spent my hours in play,
  And my heart was full of love.

I loved the heath-clad hill,
  And I loved the silent vale,
With its dark and purling rill
  That murmured in the gale.

Of sighs—I'd none to spare,—
  They were stored for riper years,
When I drained the dregs of care
  With many bitter tears.

My simple daily fare
  In my little tiny mug,
How fain was I to share
  With poor Cato on the rug.
Yes,—he gave his honest paw,
  And he licked my happy face;
He was true to Nature's law,
  And I thought it no disgrâce.

There's a voice so soft and clear,
  And a step so gay and light,
That charms my listening ear
  In the visions of the night;
And my Father bids me haste,
  In the deep fond tones of love,
To leave this dreary waste
  For brighter realms above.

Now, I am old and grey,
  My bones are racked with pain,
And time speeds fast away—
  But why should I complain?
There are joys in life's young morn,
  That dwell not with the old,
Like flowers the wind hath torn
  From the stem,—all bleak and cold.

The weary heart may mourn
  O'er the withered joys of youth,
But the flowers so rudely shorn
  Still leave the seeds of truth :—
And there's hope for hoary men,
  When they're laid beneath the sod—
For we'll all be young again
  When we meet around our God!

SING ME THE SONGS I LOVE.

JOHN READE.

Sing me the songs I love, once more,
  The songs your lips have made so dear,
For many a day must pass before
  Again your music fills my ear.
And when you are no longer near,
  I'll, in my loneliness, rejoice,
Deep in my inmost heart, to hear
  The gentle music of your voice.

'Tis not in words that friendship lies,
  E'en when those words in music move;
But words have power that never dies,
  When said or sung by those we love.
So, when in weariness I rove
  Through the world's desert, seeking rest,
The memory of your songs shall prove
  A solace to my lonely breast.

And when you sing those songs again,
  For gayer hearts and brighter eyes,
And thinking upon "now" as "*then*,"
  Memories of other days arise,
Believe that none more dearly prize
  The strains your lips so sweetly pour,
Than he who asked 'neath other skies
  "Sing me the songs I love, once more."

MY COUSIN.

D. J. WALLACE.

I have a gentle cousin,
  A fair and laughing maid,
Whose presence is my sunshine,
  Whose absence is my shade.
When sadness o'er my feelings
  Has thrown its gloomy pall,
Her soft and sunny eye-beam
  Soon banishes it all.

She's grander than the lily,
  And gayer than the rose,
As glad as morning sunshine,
  Yet spotless as the snows;
She's gentle as an angel,
  And trusting as a dove—
A brighter earthly being
  Was never formed to love.

I know not why it is so,
  Yet always round my heart
Her presence throws a gladness
  With which I would not part.
I seek her out at even,
  When weary all the day,
Then how like clouds of heaven
  The moments melt away!

She always loves what I do,
  No matter what it be;
I blame her for this sameness
  While she is blaming me.
We often read together,
  My choice is always hers—
There's not a book I cherish
  But that she, too, prefers.

We sing together sometimes—
  Her voice is like a spell;
Within her tones all trembling
  What heavenly numbers dwell!
The music of the mermaid,
  Soft echoing from the shore,—
Though I have never heard it,
  Could not delight me more.

We wander through the forest,
  When autumn leaves are strewn,
And hear, with pleasing sadness,
  The low wind's pensive moan;

And talk of joyous moments
  That have too quickly passed,
For our hearts have learned the lesson
  That pleasures cannot last.

And through the wood we wander,
  When first the spring comes on
To clothe the leafless branches
  In verdure all its own;
Then if our sky is clouded,
  As sometimes it may be,
Hope, in our hearts reviving,
  Bids every shadow flee.

'Tis thus my gentle cousin
  Sheds joy around my way,
And scatters, with profusion,
  Bright flowers where'er I stray.
I feel her influence round me,
  Like some deep-hidden spell,
And though I've other cousins,
  There's none I love so well.

THE ANGELS OF THE BLIND.

JAMES M'CARROLL.

Though on the dark, drear walls of the lonely blind man's skull
  A picture's never hung by the glowing hand of Light,
But in the gloomy catacomb his brain beats, thick and dull,
  Like some huge lazy death-watch slowly wearing out the night;

And though along the pavement of that cavern never pours
  One beam of all the beauty or the life that 'round us teems,
And Nature, as in wantonness, has shut its outer doors,
  And almost made a desert of the very land of dreams;

Yet, there are viewless angels that surround him night and day,
  Who sport throughout that sepulchre as if it were a grove,
And though he never sees them, still he hears their wings at play,
  And knows they are the voices of the ones he learned to love.

"LITTLE WILLIE."

SAMUEL PAYNE FORD.

" Good night, dear Willie," his mother said,
As she laid him down in his cradle bed,
And folded the coverlet, soft and warm,
Around his delicate little form.

" Good-night, mamma," the child replied,
As his mother bent o'er the cradle side,
And, clasping her arms around his neck,
Imprinted a kiss on her darling's cheek;

While her beating heart, uplifted high,
With all of a mother's fervency,
Sought aid of an All-sufficient arm
To shield her innocent boy from harm.

The morning has dawned, as oft before;
The robins are chirping around the door;
And often in wonder his mother hath said,
" What keeps little Willie so long in his bed?

"Come, Willie, dear Willie!" aloud she cries,
And "Willie" the echo alone replies;
Then, softly approaching his little bed,
She places her hands on his curly head.

Ah! mother, no sound in the little room
Was heard in the midnight hours of gloom,
For an angel band had softly borne
Thy Willie away to a brighter morn.

A smile still plays on his ruby lips,
But his eyes are darkened in death's eclipse;
The beautiful curls still shine like gold,
But the heart is still, and the form is cold.

FAREWELL.

MRS. FAULKNER.

Go, and God speed thee! sundered wide may be
Our future paths through life,—and yet, and yet,
Though our lone dwelling may be far from thee,
Yet, wheresoever turn thy footsteps free,
Wilt thou forget?

Wilt thou forget? when round thine *own* hearth beaming,
Kind faces greet thee with their looks of cheer,
Those whom the bitter tears of parting streaming,
And all affection's fond and anxious dreaming,
Have made so dear?

Wilt thou forget? when, sparkling bright around thee,
Are leaf and blossom, all with dew-drops wet,
When Nature's gentle influences surround thee,
And like a holy spell their charm hath bound thee,
Wilt thou forget?

Wilt thou forget? when lowly thou art bending,
In thy still chamber's solitude, thy knee,—
When up to Heaven the low-voiced prayers ascending,
With thine *own* name, oh! will not theirs be blending,
Who pray for thee?

Wilt thou forget? No, for thy heart is thrilling
With youth's warm feelings, and thy dimmed eyes tell
Of more of grief than the proud lip is willing
To utter; go, for tears mine own are filling,
Farewell, farewell.

HOPE IN SORROW.

REV. T. CLEWORTH.

My Saviour trod the earth,
Within her folds he lay;
And he shall raise to second birth
This lifeless form of clay.

Consign it to the dust,
Weep o'er it gushing tears,
But leave the pledge in Jesu's trust,
Until he re-appears.

Fair in its youthful dress
The faded floweret lies;
The essence of its loveliness
Is garnered in the skies.

The Prince of Life will come,
And all its grace restore;
The withered bud shall rise and bloom
Upon a deathless shore.

The dewy night of tears
  Foretells the radiant morn,
When, rising from our dream of fears,
  A thousand joys are born.

The tears of earth are shed
  To gild the flowers above;
While over all the beams are spread
  Of God's restoring love.

THE BEECH-NUT GATHERER.

PAMELIA S. VINING.

All over the earth like a mantle,
  Golden, and green, and gray,
Crimson, and scarlet, and yellow,
  The Autumn foliage lay;—
The sun of the Indian-Summer
  Laughed at the bare old trees,
As they shook their leafless branches
  In the soft autumnal breeze.

Gorgeous was every hill side,
  And gorgeous every nook,
And the dry, old log was gorgeous,
  Spanning the little brook;
Its holiday robes the forest
  Had suddenly cast to earth,
And, as yet, seemed scarce to miss them
  In its plenitude of mirth.

I walked where the leaves the softest
  The brightest, and goldenest lay;
And I thought of a forest hill-side,
  And an Indian-Summer day,
An eager, little child-face,
  O'er the fallen leaves that bent,
As she gathered her cup of beech-nuts
  With innocent content.

I thought of the small brown fingers,
  Gleaning them one by one;
With the partridge drumming near her
  In the forest bare and dun,
And the jet black squirrel, winking
  His saucy jealous eye
At those tiny, pilfering fingers,
  From his sly nook up on high.

Ah! barefooted little maiden!
  With thy bonnetless, sun-burnt brow,
Thou glean'st no more on the hill-side—
  Where art thou gleaning now?
I knew by the lifted glances
  Of thy dark, imperious eye,
That the tall trees bending o'er thee
  Would not shelter thee by and by.

The cottage by the brook side,
  With its mossy roof is gone,
The cattle have left the uplands,
  The young lambs left the lawn,

Gone are thy blue-eyed sister,
  And thy brother's laughing brow,
And the beach-nuts lie ungathered
  On the lonely hill-side now.

What have the returning seasons
  Brought to thy heart since then,
In thy long and weary wand'rings
  In the paths of busy men?—
Has the Angel of grief or of gladness
  Set his seal upon thy brow?
Maiden! joyous or tearful,
  Where art thou gleaning now?

THE LIFE-FORGE.

JENNIE E. HAIGHT.

Blow the bellows--faster, faster,
  In the busy forge of life;
Heap the coals on—higher, higher,
  Sevenfold heat for sevenfold strife!

In this forge must ore be melted,
  Out of which, with curious plan,
And incessant toil, to fashion
  And build up the perfect man.

Here must thought be shaped to action,
  Passion moulded into Will,
And upon time's batter'd anvil
  Every blow be dealt with skill.

Oft the metal must be heated
  In temptation's burning glow;
Oft be cool'd in baths of sorrow
  Fill'd from founts of deepest woe.

Ere, with temper firm, yet pliant,
  Heart to feel and head to plan,
Stamp'd with God's approving impress,
  We can say, "Behold a Man!"

Blow the bellows—faster, faster,
  In the busy forge of life;
Heap the coals on—higher, higher,
  Sevenfold heat for sevenfold strife!

In this age of thought and action,
  Men are needed, true and tried;
Men, with intellect far-reaching—
  Men with souls to God allied;

Men with loyal hearts, and loving;
  Men, with willing hands and strong;
Feeling for the woes of others,
  Fighting bravely 'gainst the wrong.

When from out the smoke and clamor
  Of life's forge there spring to birth
Such men, loyal, brave and loving,
  There is hope in store for earth.

And each passing day more clearly
  Proves that there is worth in man;
That, amid earth's jar and tumult,
  God is working out his plan—

Raising up our fallen nature
  Purified from every stain,
And, by earthly toil and trial,
  Fitting it with him to reign.

SEA-SHORE MUSINGS.

MRS. J. L. LEPROHON.

How oft I've longed to gaze on thee,
  Thou proud and mighty deep!
Thy vast horizon, boundless—free—
  Thy coast so rude and steep;
And now entranced I breathless stand,
  Where earth and ocean meet,—
Thy billows wash the silver sand,
  And break around my feet.

Lovely thou art when dawn's red light,
  Sheds o'er thee its soft hue,
Showing far ships, a gallant sight,
  Upon thy waters blue;
And when the moonbeams softly pour
  Their light on wave or glen,
And diamond spray leaps on the shore,
  How lovely art thou then!

Still, as I look, faint shadows steal
  O'er thy calm, heaving breast,
And there are times I sadly feel
  Thou art not thus at rest;

And I bethink me of past tales,
  Ships that have left the shore,
And meeting with thy fearful gales,
    Have ne'er been heard of more.

They say thy depths hold treasures rare,
  Groves of coral—sands of gold—
Pearls fit but for monarch's wear,
  And gems of worth untold;
But these could not to life restore
  The idol of one home,
Nor make brave hearts beat high once more,
  Who sleep beneath thy foam.

But I must chase such thoughts away,
  They mar this happy hour,
Remembering thou dost but obey
  Thy great Creator's power—
And in my own Canadian home,
  Mysterious, boundless main,
In dreams I'll see thy snow-white foam
  And frowning rocks again.

THE ENGLISHMAN'S FAREWELL.

JOHN SCOBLE.

England, my native land, farewell!
Where'er I rove, where'er I dwell,
Dear shall thy memory be to me,
As music's richest melody:
  Queen of the sea, imperial isle,
  May Heaven on thee propitious smile!

Thy sons are brave, thy maidens fair,
Of noble race, and princely air;
The virtues of their sires they prove
In arms, in honor, and in love.
Queen of the sea, &c.

Thy laws are right, thy judges pure,
Thy statesmen wise, thy throne secure,
The slave and exile find in thee
The chosen home of liberty:
Queen of the sea, &c.

From India to the Arctic Pole,
Peoples and tribes thy laws control:
Mother of nations thou shalt be,
And own a glorious progeny:
Queen of the sea, &c.

All love and loyalty be to thee,
Thou sceptred mistress of the sea;
Bright are the records of thy fame,
And glory circles round thy name:
Queen of the sea, &c.

Health to our Sovereign lady Queen,
Long may she reign in peace serene;
Long may her people, great and free,
Extend thy power, and honor thee,
Queen of the sea, imperial isle,
May Heaven on thee forever smile!

THE NIGHT-WIND.

JOHN F. M'DONNELL.

An elfin strange is the Night-Wind,
As it sweeps o'er vale and wood,
And ripples the broad, bright mirror
Of the river's sleeping flood;
It plays in the lonely hollow—
It steals o'er the dusty ground,
And it lingers in garden alleys
With a weird and ghost-like sound;
And the pines give forth a murmur,
Like a many-voicèd prayer,
From the aisles of the forest swelling
On the wings of the evening air.

Where the lilac wreaths are densest
It plays 'mid the scented gloom;
Where the thorn blossoms cluster
It breathes a rich perfume;
In the grass of the waving meadow
It gambols wild and free;
And a store of sweets it bringeth
From the distant flowery lea;
It gathers the thousand odors
Of leaf, and tree, and flower,
To shed o'er the mystic beauty
Of the balmy vesper hour.

I stroll through the crowded city,
  And the noise of busy life,
But my heart is 'mid summer landscapes,
  Far from the din and strife;
The woods are dim and distant,—
  I cannot hear their song,
But I feel their breath on my forehead,
  When the Night-Wind sweeps along.
And oft, when the deepening twilight
  Veileth the golden west—
This world and its cares forgetting—
  I dream of a Land of Rest.

THE PEARL.

JAMES M'CARROLL.

The Seasons are but Nature's jewelled ring,
  Where, set in changing splendors, we behold
The pearly winter and the em'rald spring,
  The ruby summer and the autumn's gold
In the rich ceinture ever varying:
  And where the dazzling fingers of the sun,
That fling the tinted shuttles of the light,
  Present the jewels to us one by one,
Forever circling and forever bright;
  And where, when all the fervid heats are done,
The cool, pale pearl is turned upon our sight,
  That we may revel in a new delight,
And to our Autumn, Spring, and Summer lays,
And yet one other song of grateful praise.

THE EARTH'S COMPLAINT.

PAMELIA S. VINING.

I plucked a fair flower that grew
In the shadow of summer's green trees—
A rose-petalled flower,
Of all in the bower,
Best beloved of the bee and the breeze.
I plucked it, and kissed it, and called it my own—
This beautiful, beautiful flower,
That alone in the cool tender shadow had grown
Fairest and first in the bower.

Then a murmur I heard at my feet—
A pensive and sorrowful sound;
And I stooped me to hear,
While tear after tear
Rained down from my eyes to the ground,
As I, listening, heard
This sorrowful word,
So breathing of anguish profound:

"I have gathered the fairest and best,
I have gathered the rarest and sweetest;—
My life-blood I've given
As an off'ring to Heaven
In this flower, of all flowers the completest.
Through the long, quiet night
With the pale stars in sight—
Through the sun-lighted day
Of the balm-breathing May,

I have toiled on, in silence, to bring
    To perfection this beautiful flower—
    The pride of the blossoming bower—
The queenliest blossom of spring.

    "But I am forgotten—none heed
Me—the brown soil where it grew;
        That drank in by day
        The sun's blessed ray
And gathered at twilight the dew;—
    That fed it by day and by night
    With nectar drops slowly distilled
    In the secret alembic of earth,
    And diffused through each delicate vein,
    Till the sunbeams were charmed to remain,
    Entranced in a dream of delight—
    Stealing in with their arrows of light,
    Through the calyx of delicate green—
    The close-folded petals between
    Down into its warm hidden heart;—
    Until, with an ecstatic start
    At the rapture so wondrous and new,
    That throbbed at its innermost heart,
    Wide opened the beautiful eyes;
    And lo! with a sudden surprise,
    Caught the glance of the glorious sun—
    The ardent and worshipful one—
Looking down from his heavenly place:
    And the blush of delighted surprise
    Remained in its warm glowing dyes,
Evermore on that radiant face.

"Then mortals in worshipful mood
Bent over my wonderful flower,
And called it 'the fairest,
The richest, the rarest,
The pride of the blossoming bower.'
But I am forgotten. Ah me!
I, the brown soil where it grew;
That cherished and nourished
The stem where it flourished.
And fed it with sunshine and dew!

"O Man! will it always be thus,
Will you take the rich gifts which are given
By the tireless workers of earth,
By the bountiful Father in heaven;
And, intent on the worth of the gift,
Never think of the Maker, the Giver?—
Of the long patient effort—the thought
That secretly grew in the brain
Of the poet to measure and strain,
Till it burst on your ear richly fraught
With the wonderful sweetness of song?—

"What availeth it, then, that ye toil—
You, thought's patient producers—to be
Unloved and unprized,
Trodden down and despised,
By those whom you toil for like me—
Forgotten and trampled like me?"
Then my heart made indignant reply,
In spite of my fast falling tears—
In spite of the wearisome years

Of toil unrequited that lay
In the track of the past, and the way
Thorn-girded I'd trod in those years.

So be it, if so it *must* be!—
May I know that the thing
I so patiently bring
From the depths of the heart and the brain,
A creature of *beauty* goes forth,
'Midst the hideous phantoms that press
And crowd the lone paths of this work-weary life,
'Mid the labor and care, the temptation and strife,
To gladden, and comfort, and bless.

So be it, if so it *must* be!—
May I know that the thing
I so patiently bring
From the depths of the heart and the brain,
Goes forth, with a conqueror's might,
Through the gloom of this turbulent world;
Potent for truth and for right,
Where truth has so often been hurled
'Neath the feet of the throng,
The hurrying, passionate throng!

What matter though I *be* forgot,
Since toil is itself a delight?
Since the power to do,
To the soul that is true,
Is the uttered command of the Lord
To labor and faint not, but still
Pursue and achieve,
And ever believe
THAT ACHIEVEMENT ALONE IS REWARD!

TO MY SISTER.

SAMUEL PAYNE FORD.

I've been thinking, sister Lizzie,
  Of the happy days of yore,
When our spirit-freighted life barques
  Glided gaily out from shore;
And, with scarce a cloud above them,
  Or a ripple at their side,
Started boldly for the haven
  To be found across the tide.

And in tracing faded footsteps
  By the light that Memory lends,
I have glanced again at childhood,
  With its happy home and friends;
And the magic re-appearance
  Of each well-remembered face,
Has repaid me for returning
  To the old familiar place.

O delightful, dearest sister,
  Where those bright and happy hours,
When our atmosphere of sunshine
  Was perfumed with fragrant flowers;
And the music of the song-birds
  Singing sweetest strains of love,
Made our earth seem like a picture
  Of the Paradise above?

But we've breasted many a billow
  On life's stormy sea since then;
And borne many a fierce encounter
  With unfriendly fellow-men;
And the wailing winds have whistled
  Wildly round us like a foe,
That would bear us on, resistless,
  To some wilderness of woe.

O'er the faded forms of loved ones
  Who have passed the mystic bourne,
Whence no traveller e'er returneth
  We have oft been called to mourn.
And our parting salutations
  Have been often interchanged,
As in sunshine, or in sadness,
  O'er the wide, wide world we ranged.

But the sky is growing brighter
  As the clouds are moving past,
And beyond their "silver lining,"
  I can see the end at last;
And up near the pearly portals
  That bedeck the other side,
I behold the friends we parted from
  Away back in the tide.

And they greet us with rejoicing,
  As we hasten to the shore,
Where the sound of lamentation
  Shall assail us nevermore;
But the angels' grand "*Te Deum*,"
  And the songs of the forgiven,
Shall reverberate forever
  Through the azure vault of heaven.

SAUL STRUGGLING WITH MALZAH.

(*From* SAUL.)

CHARLES HEAVYSEGE.

Creature, begone, nor harrow me with horror!
Thine eyes are stars; oh, cover them, oh, wrap
Them up within thy cloudy brows: stand off,
Contend not with me, but say who thou art.
Methinks I know thee,—yes, thou art my demon,
Thou art the demon that tormentest me.
I charge thee, shy, mysterious visitant,
At whose behest thou comest, and for what
Offences deep of mine: nay, nay, stand off:
Confess, malicious goblin, or else leave me;
Leave me, oh goblin, till my hour is come:
I'll meet thee after death; appoint the place;
On Gilead, or beside the flowing Jordan;
Or, if parts gloomier suit thee, I'll repair
Down into Hinnom, or up to the top
Of Horeb in th' wilderness, or to the cloud-
Concealèd height of Sinai ascend,
Or dwell with thee 'midst darkness in the grave.

ACROSS THE RIVER.

MRS. P. L. HANEY.

I am standing near a river—
They tell me it is death;
Its breezes, cold and chilly,
Fan me with their icy breath.

There's a mist above its waters,
  Which stretches to the land,
Where it casts a sombre shadow
  O'er the margin where I stand.

I am drawing nearer, nearer
  To the dark descending brink,
And my flesh begins to tremble,
  Though my spirit does not shrink;
For I know across the river
  Lies a valley green and fair,
Where the pure and holy wander—
  I am longing to be there.

I am weary, weary living
  In this cloudy atmosphere,
Where the brightest eye that sparkles
  Is no stranger to a tear.
But across the river, yonder
  Where the pure and holy stray,
By the hand of the Redeemer,
  Every tear is wiped away.

Here are faces bright and winning,
  Though the heart is full of guile;
And the foe who would deceive us
  First allures us with a smile—
In the land across the river,
  Which I now in spirit view,
On the faces of the holy,
  There are smiles—but they are true.

Here how often I have parted
  With the friends I love the most—
Here my choicest vase is broken,
  And my rarest treasure lost;
In the country of the holy,
  In the land of endless day,
There my friends will never leave me,
  Nor my treasures know decay.

I am drawing nearer—nearer—
  But I shudder not nor start,
Though the billows lave my footsteps,
  And the cold spray chills my heart;
I bare my pulseless bosom
  To the cold and ruthless wave,
For the faith that nerves my spirit
  Bids defiance to the grave.

Now a light gleams o'er the waters,
  From the bright and holy land,
And the king in all his beauty
  Gently leads me by the hand;
The sting of death is over,—
  Earthly friends, a long adieu!
I am passing o'er the river,
  With the holy land in view.

DESPONDENCY.

C. SANGSTER.

There is a sadness o'er my spirit stealing,
  A flash of fire up-darting to my brain,
Sowing the seeds—and still the seeds concealing—
  That are to ripen into future pain.

I feel the germs of madness in me springing,
  Slowly, and certain as the serpent's bound,
And my poor hopes, like dying tendrils clinging
  To the green oak, tend surely to the ground;
And Reason's grasp grows feebler day by day,
  As the slow poison up my nerves is creeping,
  Ever and anon through my crushed heart leaping,
Like a swift panther darting on its prey;
  And the bright taper Hope once fed within,
  Hath waned and perished in the rueful din.

THE FALLING SNOW.

ISIDORE G. ASCHER.

Fall, like peace, O gossamer snow!
While the searching winds are roaming abroad;
Fall, in your wealth, on the world below,
  Like a blessed balm from God!

Fall like kisses upon the earth,
That is cold and cheerless, and full of woe,
And fill its heart with a sense of mirth,
  Silent and loving snow!

Fall in your wonderful purity,
Fair as a bride's unsullied dress;
Fall from the heaven's immensity,
  On our autumn dreariness.

Fall like a lover's phantasy,
That the heart of a maiden might yearn to know;
Fall like a loving memory
  On a soul o'erladen with woe.

Fall like the light of an infant's smile,
That sweetly beams for a mother alone;
Fall like hope, when it dawns awhile
On a doubting heart of stone.

Fall like tears that leave us resigned
When the soul submits to a hapless doom;
Fall like light that falls on the blind,
On a life o'er-steeped in gloom.

Fall like the bounties God has given,
While the mournful winds are piping abroad;
Fall like the hints we have of heaven,
Like a blessed balm from God!

THE RED-MEN—A SONNET.

CHARLES SANGSTER.

My footsteps press where, centuries ago,
The Red-Men fought and conquered; lost and won.
Whole tribes and races, gone like last year's snow,
Have found the Eternal Hunting Grounds, and run
The fiery gauntlet of their active days,
Till few are left to tell the mournful tale:
And these inspire us with such wild amaze,
They seem like spectres passing down a vale
Steeped in uncertain moonlight, on their way
Towards some bourn where darkness blinds the day,
And night is wrapped in mystery profound.
We cannot lift the mantle of the past:
We seem to wander over hallowed ground:
We scan the trail of Thought, but all is overcast.

ON THE RIVER.

E. H. DEWART.

The sun has gone down in liquid gold
On the Ottawa's gleaming breast;
And the silent Night has softly rolled
The clouds from her starry vest;
    Not a sound is heard,—
    Every warbling bird
Has silenced its tuneful note,
    As, with calm delight,
    In the moon's weird light,
I enter my little boat.

As down the river I dreamily glide,—
The sparkling and moonlit river,
Not a ripple disturbs the glassy tide,
Not a leaf is heard to quiver;
    The lamps of night
    Shed their trembling light,
With a tranquil and silvery glory,
    Over river and dell,
    Where the Zephyrs tell
To the Night their plaintive story.

I softly time my gleaming oar,
To the music of joy-laden strains,
Which the silent woods, and the listening shore
Re-echo in soft refrains:
    Let holy thought,
    From this faery spot

Float up through the slumbering air;
　　For who who would profane,
　　With fancies vain,
A scene so unearthly fair?

Now dark-browed sorrowful Care retires,
And leaves the bright moments unclouded—
For why should I shade them with vain desires,
For hopes which the darkness has shrouded?
　　Like phantoms grim,
　　From the river's brim,
The trees stretch their shadows before me,
　　But no shadow mars—
　　For the blessed stars
Are tenderly beaming o'er me.

On the dark, and rapid stream of life
Are shadows of grief and sin,
But we reck not the gloom of the outer strife,
If no shadows obscure within;
　　Though darkness may lower,
　　It is reft of power
Over hearts that are tempered with love,—
　　There is fadeless light,
　　For life's darkest night,
With the bountiful Father above.
In holy thought, from this blissful hour—
While free from earth's darkling strife—
I may garner joy, and be nerved with power
To fight on in the battles of life.

TO A DANDELION.

MISS H. M. JOHNSON.

Blessings on thy sunny face,
In my heart thou hast a place,
    Humble Dandelion!
Forms more lovely are around thee,
Purple violets surround thee,—
But I know thy honest heart
Never felt a moment's smart
At another's good or beauty,—
Ever at thy post of duty,
Smiling on the great and small,
Rich and poor, and wishing all
Health, and happiness, and pleasure,
O thou art a golden treasure!

I remember years ago,
How I longed to see thee blow,
    Humble Dandelion!
Through the meadows I would wander,
O'er the verdant pastures yonder,
Filling hands and filling lap,
Till the teacher's rap, rap, rap,
Sounding on the window sash
Dreadful as a thunder crash,
Called me from my world ideal,—
To a world how sad and real,—
From a laughing sky and brook,
To a dull old spelling-book;
Then with treasures hid securely,
To my seat I crept demurely.

Childhood's careless days are o'er,
Happy school days come no more,
 Humble Dandelion!
Through a desert I am walking,
Hope eluding, pleasure mocking,
Every earthly fountain dry,
Yet when thou didst meet mine eye,
Something like a beam of gladness
Did illuminate my sadness,
And I hail thee as a friend
Come a holiday to spend
By the couch of pain and anguish,
Where I suffer, moan, and languish.

When at length I sink to rest,
And the turf is on my breast,
 Humble Dandelion!
Wilt thou when the morning breaketh,
And the balmy spring awaketh,
Bud and blossom at a breath
From the icy arms of death,
Wilt thou smile upon my tomb?
Drawing beauty from the gloom,
Making life less dark and weary,
Making death itself less dreary,
Whispering in a gentle tone
To the mourner sad and lone,
Of a spring-time when the sleeper
Will arise to bless the weeper?

LULLABY.

MISS BALDWYN.

Now the night draws near,
And my Willie dear
Must be lulled to his evening rest;
While the birds fold their wings,
And the zephyr sings,
Let him sleep on his mother's breast,
Oh, Willie, sweet Willie,
Gift from above,
Like an angel of joy
From our pure home on high
He has come, and shall claim our love.

SING ON, SAD BIRD.

JAMES MACINTOSH.

Sing on, sad bird, thou lonely whip-poor-will,
It soothes my grieving breast to hear thy lay;
Each tone that floats o'er forest, vale and hill
Bids Memory gaze upon a happier day.

When Love and Hope sat on this youthful brow
And smiling vowed that we should never part,
Sing on, sad bird, they're dead and withered now,
Thy mournful notes are balm to this sad heart.

TWILIGHT AND ITS COMPANIONS.

D. J. WALLACE.

Through the small uncurtained window,
  Peers the solemn star of even,
Fairest gem of all the myriads
  That bedeck the vault of heaven!
Softly through the azure heavens,
  Fleecy clouds are gently floating;
Oft they linger as if weary,
  Or some passing wonder noting.

In the twilight, dim and dusky,
  With Night's dark'ning mantle round me,
Talk I by the dying embers
  With the spirits that surround me,
From the world of spirits coming,
  Coming ever, ever going;
Like the waters of a fountain,
  Flowing ever, ever flowing.

Through the window see them gazing,
  In the door-way see them stealing;
Now appearing in their beauty,
  Now their fairy forms concealing.
Softly through my room they wander
  Noiseless as the sleeping number
That within the quiet church-yard
  Rest in an unbroken slumber.

Spirits of the long departed,
  Spirits of the absent living,
Crowd around me joyously,
  I, to each, a welcome giving.
Who, that in the hour of stillness,
  Hath once held such strange communion,
Dare deny, or disbelieve, that
  Spirit hath with spirit union?

Bliss ecstatic! Bliss unequalled!
  What to me earth's forms and features?
What the company of mortals
  With these fair angelic creatures?
What the joys of outward being,
  What to me the sombre Real,
When compared with what I gather
  From the wonderful Ideal?

Take me not where mighty waters
  Dash o'er rocks with wild commotion;
Take me not where raging tempests
  Plough with furious force the ocean!
Leave me at the hour of twilight
  Lost in thought's intensity!
Holding converse sweet with spirit,
  Roaming through immensity!

OLD FRIENDS.

G. MARTIN.

Ah, one by one they're falling,
And from the far-off shore
I hear a faint voice calling,
"Gay mortal, smile no more."

No longer grouped together,
We sift the gold of thought;
Each grown to each a brother,
And earth with heaven inwrought.

Old scenes have lost their brightness,—
The land, the lake, the sea;—
My heart has lost its lightness,
Gray mists encompass me.

And through this sunless vapor
They glide away, fore-doomed;
Their life a blown-out taper,—
Blown out ere half consumed.

Dear lights, the mist grows colder;
The voice exclaims again:
"Thy heart is growing older,
Take rank with wiser men."

Old Friends,—in vain the warning!
I seek no comrades new;
Enough, that manhood's morning
Revealed its joy with you.

Enough that Faith reminds me,
  Your spirits wander far
Beyond the fog that blinds me,
  Above each glimmering star.

LAST WORDS OF SAUL.

(*From* SAUL.)

CHARLES HEAVYSEGE.

Now let me die, for I indeed was slain
With my three sons. Where are ye, sons? Oh let me
Find ye, that I may perish with you; dying,
Cover you with my form, as doth the fowl
Cover her chickens! Oh, Philistia
Thou now art compensated,—now are getting
Rich with this crimson, hot, and molten tide;
That waits not patient to be coined in drops,
But rushes, in an ingot-forming stream,
Out of the mine and mintage of my heart!
Oh my three poor dead sons, where are you? Ye
Have gone before me into the hereafter
Upon such innocency-flighted steps.
That I, with feet cumbered with clots of blood,
Shall lose of you all glimpse, and then my soul
Shall drop to the abyss. Gush faster, blood,
And gallop with my soul towards Hades,
That yawns obscure.

BROKEN REEDS.

MRS. RHODA A. FAULKNER.

"Mine shall be glory," the warrior said,
As away to the battle-field he sped,
And proudly floated his snowy plume,
As he hied him onward to meet his doom.
"Mine shall be glory" at morn he said,
And at eve he lay with the nameless dead;
Untold, unsung, is each daring deed,
Warrior! thy hope—was a Broken Reed.

"They shall speak of my fame in a distant age,
I shall charm the world with my glowing page,
When I am low in the silent dust,
They shall rear my trophy, and carve my bust."
Minstrel! thine is a well-sung lay,
But the world shall fling it in scorn away;
And the sneer of the critic shall be thy meed,
Thou hast put thy trust in a Broken Reed.

"Heap higher, higher, the growing hoard,
My barns are full, and my coffers stored;
Ha, ha! they may call me weak and old,
But a mighty power is the power of gold,
It shall build a proud and a stately home."
Fool! it shall buy thee a costly tomb;
Vainly the learnèd leech is fee'd,
Thou hast pinned thy faith to a Broken Reed.

The proud sire looks on his gallant boy,
His manhood's darling, his age's joy.
" He shall be the staff of my year's decline,
He shall be the first of a noble line."
Old man ! thou shalt live to see them spread
" Ashes to ashes," upon his head,
The fiat is spoken, the doom decreed,
Father ! weep for thy Broken Reed.

The joy-bells ring from the ivied tower,
A merry peal for the bridal hour,
Fond lips are breathing the marriage vow,
Oh ! could they be ever as fond as now.
But the carking cares of the world will come,
And frowns will darken the happiest home ;
And each may prove, in their hour of need,
That earthly love is a Broken Reed.

Yea, Gold, and Glory, and Love, and Fame,
The tale that they tell is still the same,
The best and brightest must fade and change,
And death *will* sunder, and time estrange ;
Fix not on earth thy hope or love ;
Set thine affections on things above,
So, from the world's dark bondage freed,
Thou shalt lean no more on a Broken Reed.

TO MY LYRE.

ROBERT SWEENEY.

From thee, my Lyre, as one who bids adieu
To some dear friend he ne'er again shall meet—
Some friend whose counsel kind and converse sweet
Had shed a charm o'er moments as they flew,
Which else had loitered on with leaden feet—
From thee I part in sorrow. Thou, to me,
Didst oft, in woe, thy soothing influence lend;
Amid the wilds thou wast society,
Among the faithless thou wast still a friend.
But the world calls me from thee, and we part,
And to another's touch thy chords must swell;
No more their tones shall vibrate through my heart,
No more my ear must listen to their spell;
Farewell, beloved Lyre—till brighter hours, farewell!

January 1826.

REST.

JENNIE E. HAIGHT.

The twilight comes, the daylight goes,
The moon climbs o'er the hill;
And through the din of earthly woes
Falls Christ's own "Peace, be still!"

O weary hands! O aching heart!
O tired and throbbing brain!
How fares it with thee as the night
Sweeps by with starry train?

O hands that lovingly have toiled
Since morn's first gleam of light!
O hands by honest labor soiled,
Soft-folded, rest to-night!

O heart, with many an anguish rent,
With many a sorrow sore;
O heart, with life's fierce conflict spent—
Rest! for the day is o'er.

O brain, o'ertasked with ceaseless strain
To make time's problem clear;
O brain, deep-questioning, full of doubt,
Rest! for God reigneth here.

O friendly hands and loving heart,
And ever busy brain!
The restful night is now, but soon
The morn will dawn again.

And we must wake and work life's work,
While time's brief years may stay;
Still looking for the night of death,
And Heaven's eternal day.

There every questioning doubt shall cease,
There toil no longer tire,
And God, the triune God divine,
Fill all the soul's desire.

Oh heavenly Rest! O holy Rest!
From every conflict here
I turn to thee, with bright'ning hope,
And hail thee drawing near.

THE END.

Index of Titles

Index of Authors